WEAPON

THE BREN GUN

NEIL GRANT

Series Editor Martin Pegler

OSPREY PUBLISHING
Bloomsbury Publishing Plc

Kemp House, Chawley Park, Oxford OX2 9PH, UK
29 Earlsfort Terrace, Dublin 2, Ireland
1385 Broadway, 5th Floor, New York, NY 10018, USA
Email: info@ospreypublishing.com
www.ospreypublishing.com

OSPREY is a trademark of Osprey Publishing Ltd

First published in Great Britain in 2013
Transferred to digital print in 2016

© Osprey Publishing Ltd, 2013

A catalog record for this book is available from the
British Library.

Print ISBN: 978 1 78200 082 2
ePDF: 978 1 78200 083 9
ePub: 978 1 78200 084 6

Index by Fionbar Lyons
Battlescenes by Peter Dennis
Typeset in Sabon and Univers
Originated by PDQ Media, Bungay, UK
Printed and bound in India by Replika Press Private Ltd.

MIX
Paper from
responsible sources
FSC
www.fsc.org   FSC® C016779

24 25 26 27 28   10 9 8 7 6 5 4 3 2

The Woodland Trust
Osprey Publishing supports the Woodland Trust, the UK's
leading woodland conservation charity.

www.ospreypublishing.com
To find out more about our authors and books visit our
website. Here you will find extracts, author interviews, details
of forthcoming events and the option to sign-up
for our newsletter.

Dedication
For my best Weasel.

Acknowledgements
The author and editor would like to thank the staff and trustees
of the Small Arms School Corps museum for their invaluable
assistance in the preparation of this book.

Imperial War Museum Collections
Many of the photos in this book come from the Imperial War
Museum's huge collections which cover all aspects of conflict
involving Britain and the Commonwealth since the start of the
twentieth century. These rich resources are available online to
search, browse and buy at www.iwmcollections.org.uk. In
addition to Collections Online, you can visit the Visitor Rooms
where you can explore over 8 million photographs, thousands of
hours of moving images, the largest sound archive of its kind in
the world, thousands of diaries and letters written by people in
wartime, and a huge reference library. To make an appointment,
call 020 7416 5320.
Email: mail@iwm.org.uk
Imperial War Museum website: www.iwm.org.uk

Editor's note
For ease of comparison please refer to the following
conversion table:

1 mile = 1.6km
1yd = 0.9m
1ft = 0.3m
1in = 2.54cm/25.4mm
1lb = 0.45kg

Artist's note
Readers may care to note that the original paintings from which
the battlescenes of this book were prepared are available for
private sale. All reproduction copyright whatsoever is retained by
the Publishers. All enquiries should be addressed to:

Peter Dennis, 'Fieldhead', The Park, Mansfield,
Nottinghamshire NG18 2AT, UK

Email: magie.h@ntlworld.com

The Publishers regret that they can enter into no correspondence
upon this matter.

Image acknowledgements
Front cover images: (top) Mk II Bren with Mk I components,
courtesy of Rock Island Auction Company; (bottom) Norwegian
troops training with the Bren (IWM H 11121).

Title page image: Practising engaging aircraft by the somewhat
optimistic so-called 'hose-pipe method' during training, 1942.
(IWM H 18721)

CONTENTS

INTRODUCTION

The machine gun first appeared in the last decades of the 19th century, but it was during World War I that it came of age. The few guns initially issued to each battalion multiplied as they proved their value; a typical British Army infantry battalion began the war with two machine guns in 1914, but would field 36 machine guns by the time it ended in 1918, with further guns in the separate dedicated battalions of the Machine Gun Corps.

Indeed, the battlefields of World War I were shaped both physically and tactically by artillery and the machine gun, which forced troops underground in order to survive, while assaults were preceded by massive bombardments intended to suppress enemy machine guns. They were often unsuccessful in doing so, and machine-gun teams emerged from their deep dugouts immediately the barrages lifted to put down killing fire on the lines of infantry struggling forward. Infantrymen joked grimly that it was no longer 'the bullet with your name on it' that would get you, but one of the tens of thousands marked 'To whom it may concern'.

World War I saw machine guns diversify in type as well as increase in number. While the British Vickers was probably the best and most sophisticated design, several of the combatant nations had started the war with very similar guns – essentially slightly different versions of the heavy, water-cooled Maxim. These guns were ideal for defence, and sophisticated tactics evolved which even allowed their highly trained crews to use them for indirect fire, like artillery.

However, these guns were essentially immobile, and there was an increasing need for a lighter weapon that could go forward with the advancing infantry and provide mobile supporting fire. Some attempts to produce such guns were more successful than others. The German MG 08/15 was simply a lightened version of their standard water-cooled Maxim gun, for example; it was awkward to carry and unbalanced to use, and at 24.3kg (53lb 9oz) including a full water jacket and ammunition belt, much too heavy. The French Chauchat CSRG was chronically unreliable, particularly the .30-06 calibre version produced for US troops.

The Lewis gun used by the British and Americans was probably the best of the World War I light guns – it was so good that the Germans actually set up a production line to re-chamber captured examples to fire German ammunition, and trained their machine-gunners in their use – but even so, it was still complex, bulky and prone to stoppages.

After the war ended, the large stock of existing weapons and cuts in funding caused by the Great Depression meant that there was little chance for the British Army to develop new designs until well into the 1930s. When work began seriously on a new weapon, however, the specification was extremely ambitious. The new gun should be light and portable enough to do the job of the Lewis gun, but still able to fulfil the sustained-fire role of the heavier Vickers.

In fact, the weapon that was finally adopted – the Bren gun, a derivative of the Czech Zb 26 – fulfilled the specification brilliantly. It went through four separate versions during World War II, as it was adapted to increase production or meet changing tactical needs. While it never completely replaced the Vickers, it did serve as the primary support weapon for British and Commonwealth troops through both World War II and Korea, and set British small-unit infantry tactics on a path that they would follow until the 1980s.

An Australian Bren gunner on patrol in northern New Guinea, June 1944. (Australian War Memorial 017342)

It was not a perfect weapon, particularly as a vehicle and anti-aircraft gun, and it was perhaps fortunate for its users that circumstances minimized the effects of these shortcomings. On the other hand, it offered probably a better compromise solution than any other Allied machine gun of the period. Re-chambered for a new cartridge after the Korean War, it served briefly alongside the L1A1 SLR (Self-Loading Rifle), the British version of the Belgian FN FAL rifle, before being replaced by a version of the excellent Belgian FN MAG General Purpose Machine Gun (GPMG). Even then, the Bren remained in service as a second-line weapon for decades, seeing use in the Falklands and other small wars before finally being phased out after the 1st Gulf War, a total of more than 60 years of service.

As well as for British and Commonwealth armies, the Bren was used to arm an amazingly wide array of other forces, from the French Resistance to the Nationalist Chinese, while captured examples were used by the Germans and a substantial number of postwar insurgents.

The Bren was extremely popular with the men who had to carry it into battle, or even during peacetime. Almost all regarded it as a reliable and effective weapon, and it was striking that when discussing the Bren with veterans who had used it, their first response was almost always the same – a nostalgic smile, and the words 'It was a great gun, the old Bren...' or something similar. This is in stark contrast to soldiers' reminiscences about the other major British automatic weapon of the period, the Sten 'machine carbine' (submachine gun), which was generally despised for its poor build quality and unpleasant habit of going off on full-automatic if dropped.

A slightly fuller analysis of the Bren's strengths and weaknesses comes from the writer George MacDonald Fraser, who served in an infantry section of 9th Border Regiment in the Burma campaign during World War II:

> It was a good gun, but needed intelligent handling, for when held firm it was accurate enough to punch a hole in a brick wall with a single magazine, and to get a good spread the gunner had to fan it about judiciously. It could also be fired from the hip, given a firm stance, for without one it would put you on your back. (Fraser 1993: 32)

With its distinctive curved, top-mounted magazine, it was extremely recognizable even for civilians, and attracted a certain amount of fame – Noel Coward even produced a hit song called 'Could You Please Oblige Us with a Bren Gun?', which must have been the only popular record to name-check a specific automatic weapon until the advent of rap music.

DEVELOPMENT
How a Czech gun became a British icon

BEFORE THE BREN

Great Britain ended World War I with two primary machine guns, intended for very different tactical roles. The Vickers medium machine gun (MMG) was a relatively heavy Maxim-derived weapon. Water-cooled and belt-fed, it was a supremely reliable weapon which could lay down a solid curtain of fire as long as it had ammunition and cooling water. On one occasion in August 1916, ten Vickers guns carried out a continuous suppressing barrage for 12 hours, firing nearly a million rounds between them, without a single serious stoppage. The Lewis light machine gun was adopted during World War I, and was intended to be light enough to be carried forward to provide the advancing troops with fire support. It had an air-cooled barrel, enclosed in a tubular cooling shroud, and fired from a 47-round pan magazine mounted on top of the weapon.

Both weapons were probably the best designs in their respective classes, and clearly better than (for example) their German equivalents, the MG 08 and MG 08/15. However, both had disadvantages. The Vickers was a complex weapon requiring a specially trained crew, and the weight of the gun and its prodigious demand for water and ammunition meant that it was essentially restricted to a static defensive role, rather than the more mobile warfare anticipated for future conflicts. Meanwhile, the lighter Lewis was still relatively bulky, complicated, suffered from a relatively high rate of stoppages and its fixed barrel meant that it could not conduct real sustained fire without overheating to the point where it simply stopped working.

The British Army therefore wanted to replace the Lewis at the very least, and ideally both guns, with a single weapon. In 1922 the Small

Arms Committee (SAC) recommended adopting a version of the American Browning Automatic Rifle (BAR), to be called the Browning Light Machine Gun, apparently on grounds of better portability and reliability than the Lewis gun. However, this plan was never put into action, presumably either because of reluctance to spend more money on weapons so soon after World War I, or because the Army realized that the fixed barrel and 20-round magazine of the BAR would limit its effectiveness in sustained fire. Since the Army already had adequate weapons in place – albeit somewhat ageing and often hard used – the search for a replacement machine gun does not seem to have been pursued with any particular urgency. Five weapons (the BAR, Lewis, Beardmore-Farquhar, Hotchkiss and Madsen) were tested in December 1922, but although the BAR was preferred, nothing further happened.

The Vickers gun – dating from World War I, it was an excellent sustained-fire weapon, but not designed to provide fire support on the move. (Author)

A Lewis gun. Although probably the best of the World War I light machine guns, the Lewis was still heavy, bulky and only somewhat reliable. It fired the same .303 round as the Bren, from a 47-round pan magazine. (Author)

Over the next few years, a number of weapons were tested as they became available; a revised version of the Beardmore-Farquhar in 1924, the French Chatellerault M1924 in 1925, the Swiss Furrer and the Australian McCrudden in 1926, the Norwegian Eriksen in 1927, the Madsen (again) in 1928 and a revised version of the BAR re-chambered for the British .303in round in 1929. Nothing came of any of these tests, and they seem to have been conducted more to keep abreast of new developments than as part of a serious procurement programme.

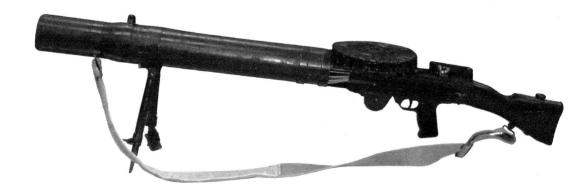

The Czech connection

The state of Czechoslovakia emerged from the wreckage of the Austro-Hungarian Empire at the end of World War I. The new nation immediately found itself surrounded by other new states, some of them with competing territorial claims, and with a wildly mismatched national arsenal. In addition to Steyr-Mannlicher rifles and Schwarzlose machine guns left over from the old Austro-Hungarian Army, the new state had substantial stocks of captured Italian and Russian weapons, plus purchased war-surplus German Mausers and large amounts of equipment brought back by the various 'Czech Legions' that formed the core of the new army. These had been raised from Czech prisoners of war, most notably by the Russians, but also by the French and Italians, who each created and armed their own legions to fight for them in return for promises of Czech independence. To make matters worse, the Czech Legion raised by the Russians had been equipped largely with captured Japanese weapons, and brought back so many 6.5mm Arisaka rifles that the Czechs thought it was worthwhile to set up a production line to make ammunition for them.

Amid this logistic nightmare, the Czechs began to build a new army. It was heavily influenced by Czechoslovakia's main ally, France, to the extent that the French Military Attaché, General Eugène Mittelhauser,

The Czech Zb 30. Note the ribbed barrel, straight 20-round magazine and the location of the gas plug, much closer to the muzzle than on the Bren. (Author)

The Czech arms industry

Czech military innovations in this period were not confined to small-arms production; their LT 35 and LT 38 light tanks were significantly better armed than their German counterparts (the PzKpfw I and PzKpfw II, respectively), and in the case of the LT 38, quickly acquired a reputation for reliability. Unfortunately, this excellent equipment proved to be of little use in defending Czechoslovakia; when the British and French failed to back the Czechs during the Munich Crisis of 1938, the territorial concessions the Czechs were forced to give up to Germany (including its painstakingly prepared frontier defences and key industrial areas) left them unable to resist complete dismemberment by the Germans early in the following year.

This gave the German forces a treasure trove of captured high-quality equipment; LT 35 and LT 38 tanks (known as the PzKpfw 35(t) and PzKpfw 38(t), respectively, in German service) formed a significant part of the German tank force during the invasions of Poland and France, and the latter vehicle continued to serve until the end of World War II as the base chassis for the *Marder III* and *Hetzer* tank destroyers. The Germans kept the Czech arms industry in full production throughout the war, and afterwards it was able to re-establish itself as one of the key arms-manufacturing countries of the Warsaw Pact. Then, the excellence of Czech design was again demonstrated by the fact that Czechoslovakia was the only Pact country whose troops were not armed with the Soviet-designed AK-series assault rifles, instead using the locally designed Vz 58 – visually similar, but significantly different internally.

actually served as Chief of the Czech General Staff. It was unsurprising, therefore, that Czech tactical organization was based on the French model, with 13-man squads grouped around a light machine gun, and equally unsurprising that Mittelhauser championed the French Darne design over other available weapons such as the Danish Madsen, despite issues of reliability. Local arms producers were not idle, however, including the three Holek brothers who produced a series of innovative designs, including the ZH-29 semi-automatic rifle. With limited resources, and with their factory on the verge of bankruptcy, they produced a series of air-cooled light machine guns. The first prototypes were belt-fed, but evolved into lighter, magazine-fed weapons, ultimately becoming the Zb 26. The Zb 26 (and the improved Zb 30) were adopted by the Czech Army, and were widely exported; in fact, more were sold to foreign purchasers than to the Czech Army, and the latter complained that its deliveries were being delayed by commercial sales.

The 1930 trials and the Zb 26

Following the inconclusive tests of the late 1920s, in 1930 Britain's SAC was formally directed to find 'a light machine gun which is capable of combining the functions of the present Vickers .303-inch machine gun and those of the present [i.e. Lewis] light automatic' (War Office 1930). A trial was quickly scheduled, to re-test the .303in conversion of the BAR and two different versions of the Madsen, along with several new weapons, including the British-made Vickers-Berthier, the French Darne, the Swiss Kiralyi-Ende, and the Zb 26 produced by the Czech Brno firm. All were relatively light air-cooled, magazine-fed weapons. The last two weapons were chambered for 7.92mm Mauser, the commonest European rifle cartridge, while the remainder were chambered for the British .303in round. A Lewis gun of the current pattern was put through the same tests, to act as a 'control weapon'.

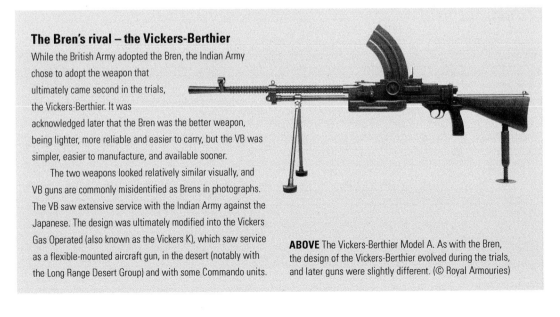

The Bren's rival – the Vickers-Berthier

While the British Army adopted the Bren, the Indian Army chose to adopt the weapon that ultimately came second in the trials, the Vickers-Berthier. It was acknowledged later that the Bren was the better weapon, being lighter, more reliable and easier to carry, but the VB was simpler, easier to manufacture, and available sooner.

The two weapons looked relatively similar visually, and VB guns are commonly misidentified as Brens in photographs. The VB saw extensive service with the Indian Army against the Japanese. The design was ultimately modified into the Vickers Gas Operated (also known as the Vickers K), which saw service as a flexible-mounted aircraft gun, in the desert (notably with the Long Range Desert Group) and with some Commando units.

ABOVE The Vickers-Berthier Model A. As with the Bren, the design of the Vickers-Berthier evolved during the trials, and later guns were slightly different. (© Royal Armouries)

Several examples of each weapon were tested for accuracy, reliability and handling, though the French Darne guns arrived too late for inclusion. Meanwhile, the Czechs had actually sent slightly improved Zb 27 guns for testing, rather than the Zb 26 models originally proposed. No further trials were recommended for the BAR or the Kiralyi-Ende, while the Madsen, Vickers-Berthier and the Brno Zb 27 were felt to be worth taking forward for more trials. The Zb 27 was the best performer, with the official report commenting 'I doubt whether any other gun has ever passed through so many tests with us, giving so little trouble' (SAC 1108). The report on the Vickers-Berthier was not so positive, but concluded 'Properly developed it should be the equal of the Zb gun' (SAC 1108).

The SAC understandably wanted to know whether the Zb gun would perform as well when chambered for British .303in ammunition, and arranged for several guns to be converted for further testing. The weapon actually converted was a Zb 30, a revised model incorporating improvements over the Zb 27 to allow it to handle the heavier-bullet Mauser cartridge recently introduced by the Germans. The converted Zb 30, one version of the Madsen and an improved model of the Vickers-Berthier were then put through further trials in 1931, including long-range shooting and a 30,000-round endurance test, along with the late-arriving Darne guns. Neither the Madsen nor the Darne was felt to justify further trials. Again, however, the resulting report was very positive about the Zb gun, described as 'of such outstanding design, workmanship and material as to warrant further serious consideration' (SAC 1188).

The SAC agreed a number of further modifications, including changes to the gas system and ejection port to reduce excessive fouling caused by changing from nitrocellulose-based Mauser ammunition to the cordite propellant used in British cartridges, and the introduction of a 30-round magazine to replace the original 20-round design. Because the British .303in rounds used a rimmed cartridge case, unlike the rimless Mauser cartridge, this magazine had a very distinctive curve rather than the straight magazine of the original 7.92mm Zb guns.[1] This curved magazine would become a highly recognizable feature of the weapon.

The committee ordered ten examples of the improved gun (known as the ZGB) for further testing and modification, including a recoil buffer in the butt, resulting in the ZGB 32. This went through further modifications, the most notable of which was the removal of the radiator fins on the barrel. Although these did allow the barrel to cool itself more quickly by increasing its surface area, the effect was small and did not justify the extra manufacturing complexity. In addition, the grooves between the fins tended to trap gun oil, which burnt off as the barrel heated up, creating a

---

1   A cartridge is normally described by its calibre, either in inches (e.g. .303in) or millimetres (e.g. 7.62mm). However, not all cartridges of the same calibre are necessarily interchangeable. For example, the FN FAL and the Soviet AK-47 both use 7.62mm rounds, but the cartridge for the former is considerably longer and will not fit the latter weapon. For clarity, and to allow comparison between cartridges usually described in imperial measurements with those generally described in millimetres, this book gives the common name (e.g. 7.62mm NATO) then the cartridge-case dimensions in millimetres (7.62×51mm, in that case). Rimmed cartridges have a pronounced flange at the bottom of the cartridge case, to be gripped by the weapon's extractor. Rimless cartridges have a groove just above the bottom of the case, effectively creating a 'rim' for the extractor to grip without increasing the diameter of the case.

Bren training in England, 1941. These troops are actually Norwegian volunteers equipped by the British. (Imperial War Museum H 11121)

heat haze and even smoke which did little to improve aiming. The resulting weapon was designated as the ZGB 33, and one of these guns fired over 140,000 rounds without any parts failing.

A few final modifications, to increase breech lock time and reduce the rate of fire slightly, produced the ZGB 34, though this term was used erratically and some documents still refer to these guns as ZGB 33s. A final 50,000-round endurance test in August 1934 compared two of these weapons with the latest heavy-barrelled version of the Vickers-Berthier. Based on the results, the Army adopted the Czech gun. Agreements were signed, and the gun was named the BREN, from 'BRno' and 'ENfield'. The drawings were converted from metric to imperial by January 1935, and the British production line was set up at Enfield, with the first gun completed in September 1937.

Overall, the testing process was extremely thorough, and the Zb models came through it with flying colours. One of the tests required a single gun to fire 150,000 rounds, a very tall order for any weapon. In fact, the test was ended after 146,802 rounds had been fired, the Ordnance Board report stating 'The gun was functioning as well at the end of the trial as it was at the beginning and there was no object to be gained from extending the trial' (SAC 1544).

The Indian Army had also been interested in the trials. However, they chose to adopt the Vickers-Berthier in 1933 without waiting for the British Army's decision, apparently because they wanted to replace their worn-out stock of Lewis guns as quickly as possible and the Vickers-Berthier was available immediately, whereas they would have to wait several years for the Bren to enter production. In fact, the Vickers-Berthier gave the Indian Army reasonable if uninspired service until eventually replaced by the Bren during World War II.

Interestingly, the very best results were obtained with the 7.92mm versions of the Zb, as the rimless rounds were inherently easier to feed in an automatic weapon than the rimmed British .303in rounds. This was a well-understood issue, and the SAC looked quite seriously into the possibility of adopting 7.92mm Mauser as a calibre for all machine guns. However, it was felt to be more important that the section light machine gun (LMG) and its supporting riflemen should use the same ammunition and there was no realistic possibility of replacing the hundreds of thousands of .303in rifles already in service.

THE .303in BRENS

The Mk I

The original Bren gun was designated the Mk I. It was a gas-operated weapon, tapping off propellant gas from a fired cartridge to drive back the gas piston and re-cock the weapon for the next shot. It was capable of semi- or full-automatic fire, from a distinctive top-mounted 30-round magazine. It had a quick-change barrel, allowing it to keep up sustained fire much longer than a comparable weapon with a fixed barrel, such as the Lewis or BAR. This could be changed in a matter of seconds without tools by a well-trained crew, and replaced by a spare barrel carried by the No. 2, allowing the weapon to continue firing while the first barrel cooled.

Why was the Bren designed for magazine rather than belt feed?

For someone used to modern belt-fed GPMGs, it is perhaps surprising that a machine gun would feed from a box magazine of limited capacity. This is partly because in the 1930s, machine guns were not seen as a single class, but two. Most armies followed the World War I pattern, with a 'heavy' gun such as the Vickers (belt-fed, relatively immobile and often water-cooled) intended for sustained fire to defend fixed positions, and a 'light' gun such as the Lewis gun or BAR, optimized for portability over sustained fire.

This was reinforced by most belt-fed guns of the period using non-disintegrating fabric belts. While these posed no problem in a static role, they were difficult to use while advancing, as the expended belt trailed from the gun, catching on obstacles and tangling the gunner's legs. Modern disintegrating link belts were in use (primarily in aircraft guns, where the fabric belts freezing solid at altitude had been an issue), but the British Army had no desire to complicate logistics by adopting a second type of belt, incompatible with the existing fabric belt used by the Vickers.

The major exception to this thinking was in Germany, where the MG 34 and MG 42 designs both used metallic non-disintegrating link belts. These weapons represented the first examples of the modern GPMG, capable of taking on both the heavy and light roles. This was partly a result of more advanced tactical thinking, which also led to the Blitzkrieg (lightning war) tactics the Germans were to use. However, it is also worth noting that the Treaty of Versailles, which ended World War I, confiscated almost all of Germany's existing stock of machine guns. It was thus both easier for Germany to innovate than for the other powers, with their large stock of existing guns, and also more necessary for her to do so, since she had to produce weapons for both roles as quickly as possible once rearmament started. Ultimately, the German approach proved the right one, and the Bren was replaced in British service (along with the Vickers, Browning and Besa) after the war by the GPMG, a version of the belt-fed Belgian FN MAG.

The Mk I Bren. Note the drum-type rear sight, the bipod with adjustable legs, butt with handle and buttstrap, and the stainless-steel construction of the whole foresight/gas block/flash-hider assembly. (Author)

As can be seen from the table below, it compared very favourably with the equivalent weapon of any other power of the same period. The only weapons that might have been regarded as being significantly better were the German MG 34 and MG 42, the first true GPMGs.

The Bren and its rivals

Weapon	Calibre	Magazine	Barrel	Weight (unloaded)	Rate of fire
Bren Mk II (Commonwealth)	.303in (7.7×56mm)	30-rd box	Quick-change	22lb 3oz	500rds/min
Lewis (Commonwealth)*	.303in (7.7×56mm)	47-rd pan	Fixed	26lb 0oz	550rds/min
Vickers-Berthier Mk 3 (Commonwealth)	.303in (7.7×56mm)	30-rd box	Quick-change	20lb 11oz	500rds/min
M1918A2 BAR (US)	.30-06 (7.62×63mm)	20-rd box**	Fixed	19lb 6oz	550rds/min
MAS FM 24/29 (French)	7.5×54mm	25-rd box	Fixed	8.9kg (19lb 9oz)	450rds/min
MG 34 (German)	7.92mm Mauser (7.92×57mm)	50-rd belt‡	Quick-change	12.1kg (26lb 10oz)	800–900rds/min
Type 96 (Japanese)‡‡	6.5×50mm	30-rd box	Quick-change	8.7kg (19lb 1oz)	550rds/min
DP (Soviet)	7.62×54mm	47-rd pan	Fixed	8.5kg (18lb 11oz)	600rds/min
MG 42 (German)	7.92mm Mauser (7.92×57mm)	50-rd belt	Quick-change	11.6kg (25lb 8oz)	1,200rds/min

*   The Lewis was also in US service, chambered for the same .30-06 round as the BAR.
**   All versions of the BAR featured a bottom-mounted magazine that was slower to change than the top-mounted magazines of the other designs.
‡   The MG 34 (but not the MG 42) could also feed from a special 75-rd double drum magazine, though this required replacing the top cover with a special unit that would no longer accept the standard belts.
‡‡   The Type 96 had a reputation for unreliability, due to poor tolerances. Attempts to rectify this by oiling the cartridges just meant that they picked up dirt and grit, actually worsening the problem.

Distinctive identification features of the Mk I include a drum rear sight, rear grip and shoulder strap on the butt, a bipod with adjustable legs, the use of stainless steel for the whole of the gas-block/flash-hider assembly and numerous cut-outs where extra metal was machined away to lighten the weapon. It was a carefully made weapon; assembly of each gun involved a total of 3,284 operations. This inevitably meant a high cost of production; the initial guns cost £40 each (equivalent to a real price of £2,120 or US $3,370 at the time of writing[2]), though this fell significantly with later versions. It was this gun that went to France with the British Expeditionary Force (BEF) in 1939.

The Mk I (Modified)

After the fall of France and the retreat from Dunkirk, the British Army found itself desperately short of Bren guns. Almost all of the 30,000 guns taken to France had been lost, and fewer than 2,300 remained in Britain to fight a potentially imminent German invasion. Increasing the rate of production was therefore a priority. On the other hand, making significant changes to the design would mean re-tooling the factory, with consequent loss of production while the changes were made. The Royal Small Arms Factory thus adopted a two-pronged approach to simplifying the Bren to improve production rates.

A Gurkha Bren gunner returning from patrol in Burma, August 1945. Although his gun has the distinctive drum sight of the Mk I, the simplified butt without buttstrap indicates the weapon is a Mk I (Modified). Butt handles were eventually removed even from weapons originally fitted with them; most were re-used as carrying handles for 2in mortars. (IWM SE 4467)

The Bren mechanism

The Bren is a gas-operated weapon. This means that when a round is fired, and the expanding propellant gas pushes the bullet down the barrel, some of the gas is tapped off at the gas port above the bipod. This gas then pushes a piston along the gas tube under the barrel, which unlocks the arrangement of cams which hold the breech block in place during firing, then forces the breech block and bolt to the rear and ejects the spent cartridge. As the bolt travels to the rear, it compresses the return spring in the butt, which eventually overcomes the impetus of the gas piston and begins to push the bolt forward again.

If the weapon is set to semi-automatic, or if the trigger has been released when the weapon is set to full-automatic,

the trigger catch engages at that point, holding the bolt to the rear so the cycle stops with the bolt open, allowing the chamber to air-cool until the trigger is pulled again. If the trigger is held down on automatic, the bolt goes straight forward instead, picking up another cartridge from the magazine, pushing it into the chamber and firing it, so that the cycle repeats.

Burned propellant from fired rounds can be deposited around the gas port, so that not enough gas is tapped off to drive the piston back, causing a stoppage. This can be dealt with by turning the gas port to the next largest of its four holes (often using the tip of a bullet as a tool), increasing the amount of gas tapped off.

The first approach was to produce a slightly simplified version of the current gun (the so-called 'Pattern A'). This involved no major changes to the gun or to the jigs and tools that made it, but simply omitted minor machining operations such as the various lightening cuts, the dovetail slot to mount the optional telescopic and fixed-line sights and so on. It was estimated that these simplifications would allow production to be increased by around 5 per cent. Such guns were originally to be designated 'Mk I Modified', but this nomenclature was never formally adopted, and both this version and the few surviving original-pattern guns were referred to as the Mk I.

These weapons also incorporated a revised barrel (Mk I*) and gas regulator, as a consequence of combat experience in France, where it was discovered that the fouling issues caused by the British cordite propellant had still not been fully resolved. These parts were also retrofitted to the existing Mk I guns, again without change of designation.

The Mk II

The second approach (the so-called 'Pattern B') was a much more radical redesign of the weapon from the ground up to simplify production. The main differences were:

- replacing the complicated drum rear sight of the Mk I with a simpler ladder rear sight that folded down when not in use
- replacing the original folding cocking handle with a simpler fixed design
- a redesigned butt with a simpler stamped butt plate rather than the original spring-loaded plate, no shoulder strap or rear handle
- a much simpler bipod with fixed legs rather than the adjustable length legs of the original bipod
- a new barrel assembly, with the flash eliminator and foresight assembly separate from the gas block so that only the latter component had to be machined from hard-to-work stainless steel
- a simplified gas cylinder
- further elimination or simplification of machining operations on the body.

The Mk II Bren. Note the ladder-type rear sight (folded down in this photograph), simplified bipod with non-adjustable legs, simplified butt without handle or buttstrap, and reduced use of stainless steel for the gas block only. (Author)

This produced a slightly heavier and less ergonomic weapon, but as it was estimated that these changes would increase production by around 20–25 per cent, they were approved in September 1940 and entered production in 1941 as the Mk II Bren.

The Mk I (Modified) and Mk II were the most-produced versions of the Bren, accounting for the great majority of the 500,000-odd weapons produced. They effectively remained the default models encountered until the switch from .303in ammunition, since the later marks were relatively low-production lightweight versions that supplemented rather than replaced them.

Bren guns by mark

Weapon	Calibre	Length (overall)	Length (barrel)	Weight (unloaded)
Mk I	.303in (7.7×56mm)	45.5in	25in	22lb 3oz
Mk II	.303in (7.7×56mm)	45.5in	25in	23lb 3oz
Mk III	.303in (7.7×56mm)	42.9in	22.25in	19lb 5oz
Mk IV	.303in (7.7×56mm)	42.9in	22.25in	19lb 2oz
L4A4	7.62×51mm	45.5in	25in	19lb 2oz

The Mk III

In 1943, trials were done to examine the possibility of a lightened Bren for jungle warfare and airborne use. The trials indicated that the weight could be reduced by a very impressive 4lb compared to the Mk II weapon, although some of the modifications identified were not carried into production guns, either because of concern that the lightened pieces would be too fragile in the field, or because they involved a disproportionate amount of expensive machining to gain a very small reduction in weight.

The resulting gun was standardized as the Mk III in July 1944. It was essentially a lightened version of the Mk I (Modified) gun, but fitted with

The Mk III Bren. Note shorter, lighter barrel, further simplification of the butt, and additional metal machined away to reduce weight. The Mk IV was visually very similar. (Author)

THE BREN EXPOSED

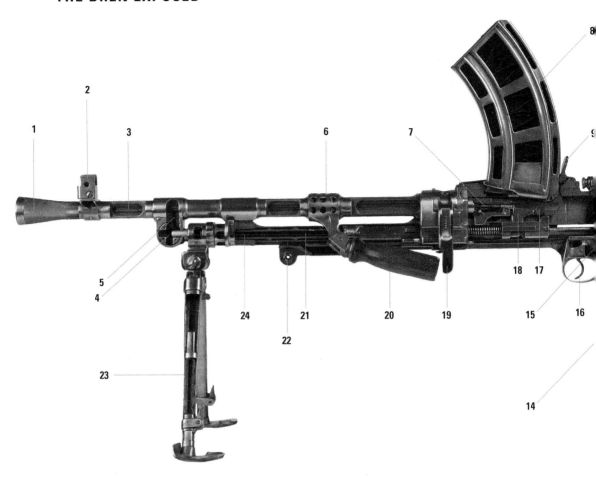

.303 Bren Mark III

1. Flash suppressor
2. Foresight
3. Barrel
4. Gas regulator
5. Gas port
6. Carrying handle sleeve
7. Firing pin
8. Magazine
9. Magazine catch
10. Rearsight (folded)
11. Body locking pin
12. Return spring
13. Butt

14. Pistol grip
15. Change lever (selector)
16. Trigger
17. Breech block
18. Piston post
19. Barrel nut
20. Carrying handle
21. Gas piston
22. Mounting pin
23. Bipod
24. Gas cylinder

(Photos © Royal Armouries, PR.1187)

Although often described as training aids, most sectioned Brens were actually produced as projects by apprentices after the Bren had left front-line service, taking advantage of the large number of surplus guns available. Given the relatively hard materials used for much of the weapon, sectioning a gun is quite a demanding task, and provided a useful project piece for students to demonstrate practical skills.

the simpler ladder back sight of the Mk II, a shorter and lighter barrel and an even simpler butt. The new barrel was some 3in shorter than the original, and slightly thinner, leading to somewhat reduced accuracy and shortened barrel life to around 7,000–10,000 rounds compared to the 12,000–15,000 rounds of the standard barrel. However, this was seen as an acceptable trade for the weight reduction. The barrels were not interchangeable between the standard and lightweight Brens. Some 57,600 Mk III Brens were produced.

The Mk IV

The Mk IV was another lightened version, but based on the Mk II rather than the Mk I. Overall, the lightening modifications were very similar to those on the Mk III, but even more metal was machined away from the body. It was standardized at the same time as the Mk III, in July 1944. However, the first guns were not issued until July 1945, and only about 250 were produced before the war ended.

The Besal gun: the emergency Bren that never was

Alongside the efforts to simplify the Bren to increase production, the Ordnance Board also proposed a much simpler weapon (the so-called 'Garage Hands Gun') that could be put into production in small workshops if Britain was invaded, or if the one factory producing the Bren was destroyed by an air raid. A minute of June 1940 set out the likely characteristics of such a gun; it would use Bren magazines and barrels, but finish, accuracy and durability could all be much poorer than the Bren, since this would be a 'last ditch' weapon. It was even proposed that since barrels were likely to be a bottleneck for production, the spare barrels from existing Bren guns could be withdrawn and used to make new guns.

Birmingham Small Arms (BSA) was given a contract to produce a prototype in 1941. There was some controversy over awarding the contract to BSA, since they were an established gun-making firm, and it was felt that asking them to produce the prototype might not be a good test of how realistically it could be produced by firms without such experience. The contract went ahead, however, and a design which became known as the Besal was submitted, with the first weapon apparently arriving at Enfield in March 1942.

The Besal gun, a simplified 'last ditch' version of the Bren. Very few examples were made, and it never went into production. (Author)

The initial weapon was a relatively straightforward design, with a conventional cocking handle. A revised design was submitted in August 1942, with a redesigned cocking system copied from the Besa tank machine gun, where the entire pistol grip went forward to catch the recoiling parts and pulled them to the rear to cock the gun. Testing showed that the gun worked efficiently enough, though it had moved rather a long way from the original 'garage workshop' concept. It was renamed the Faulkner LMG in January 1943, apparently to avoid confusion with the Besa. However, by this point the war situation had improved and the need for a Bren substitute had receded, so the Faulkner/Besal LMG was cancelled in June 1943 without entering production.

Postwar .303in upgrades

From 1948 to 1953, large numbers of wartime Mk II Brens were overhauled and refurbished at Enfield and BSA, under the Factory Thorough Repair (FTR) programme. As part of this, a number of these weapons were retrofitted with the folding cocking-handle assembly of the Mk I, and designated as Mk II/1.

WARTIME MANUFACTURING

The Mk I Bren was originally manufactured solely at RSAF Enfield, though components were manufactured by a number of suppliers organized into what was known as the 'Monotype' group. The government was very conscious that a single German air raid could destroy Britain's

Completed Brens at the Royal Small Arms Factory at Enfield. (IWM H 1573)

entire capacity to manufacture its primary LMG, however, with disastrous results. In 1938, work began to produce the Mk I Bren at the John Inglis plant in Toronto, Canada, with the first guns being completed in March 1940. By August 1942, the Inglis plant was turning out 10,000 guns per month, and produced a total of 186,000 guns during the war.

Inglis-produced Brens went through a very similar sequence of changes to the Enfield Brens, with their version of the Mk I (Modified) being marked as such (unlike the Enfield version) and being replaced by the Mk II from 1942. The Inglis plant also produced Brens in 7.92mm Mauser, for the Chinese Nationalist forces.

Production of a slightly modified version of the Mk I Bren started at the Lithgow Small Arms Factory in New South Wales, Australia, in 1940. It continued until 1945, with a total of 17,249 guns being produced. Bren production was also started at Ishapore Arsenal in India (which had previously produced the Vickers-Berthier) in 1942, and continued well after production in Britain had ended, with the final weapons actually being manufactured in 7.62mm NATO as the MG1B.

It is worth noting that not all of the changes between marks came in at the same time, and existing stocks of parts continued to be used to assemble or repair weapons after production of a new component had begun. Weapons produced in Canada and Australia also differed slightly from Enfield-made weapons, though most parts remained interchangeable; Australian-manufactured guns had a slightly different bipod design, for example.

Individual weapons might also be repaired or modified in the field or base workshops, especially to refit older Mk I guns with the improved Mk 3 gas cylinder. Such weapons may thus not fit perfectly into the marks set out above. Where guns display such a mix of features, official practice was to use the model number on the receiver. Troops in the field, however, invariably referred simply to 'Bren guns', without distinguishing between types.

Ronnie, the Bren Gun Girl. Veronica Foster, a worker on the Bren gun production line at the John Inglis plant in Toronto, Canada, became a World War II propaganda icon similar to the fictional US 'Rosie the Riveter' after being featured in a series of propaganda posters. Most of the posters showed her working for the war effort, but a few featured her at social activities such as dancing. (Libraries & Archives of Canada PA-119766)

POSTWAR DEVELOPMENTS

The EM-2 and the .280in Bren

During World War II, the Germans realized that while their standard 7.92×57mm Mauser rifle round was effective out to 600–800m (650–870yd), most firefights took place at much shorter ranges. They therefore developed a shorter version of the Mauser cartridge, the 7.92×33mm *kurz* (short), which was adequate at these shorter ranges. Because the new round had a much smaller propellant charge than the full-power rifle round, it was possible to build a practical selective-fire weapon around it, and the first assault rifle (the MP 43/StG 44) was born.

After the war, both the Soviet Union and the British built on this legacy. In the Soviet Union, Mikhail Kalashnikov created the AK-47, a 7.62×39mm assault rifle relatively similar in design to the German StG 44. The British project selected a .280in (7×43mm) cartridge which gave better range than the original German weapons while still being controllable when firing bursts. This was to be fired from a very radical assault rifle called the EM-2, which was a 'bullpup' design – a weapon with the magazine and action behind the pistol grip and trigger, rather than in front of it as in a conventional rifle. This allowed a shorter, handier weapon, without reducing barrel length.

A number of Bren guns were re-chambered to fire the new .280in round. Most were Canadian-made Inglis Mk II models, using breech blocks originally made for the 7.92mm Mauser version of the Bren produced for the Nationalist Chinese. These .280in Brens could use either the 20-round magazine of the EM-2 rifle, or a new 30-round magazine developed specifically for them. Since the .280in calibre was a rimless round, these magazines had a much-reduced curvature compared to the wartime .303in Bren magazine.

The radical .280in 'bullpup' EM-2 rifle was originally intended to replace the venerable Lee-Enfield. A small number of Brens were re-chambered to fire the same round, and the Bren would have remained in service as the standard section machine gun, with the belt-fed Taden gun for sustained fire. (Author)

The Taden gun was essentially a belt-fed version of the Bren, optimized for the sustained-fire role. This particular example was re-chambered for 7.62×51mm NATO ammunition after the abandonment of the .280in cartridge, and is also fitted with a bipod, here hinged forwards under the barrel. (© Royal Armouries PR.237/PR.238)

The design team at Enfield also developed a dedicated sustained-fire support weapon, since the change of calibre would effectively make the limited number of Vickers guns retained for the sustained-fire role obsolete. This was known as the Taden gun, and was essentially a Bren barrel and action, fitted with spade rear grips and modified for belt feed.

However, the US military establishment was unconvinced by the theory behind these so-called 'intermediate' rounds; the cartridge they wanted was the 7.62×51mm NATO, essentially a slightly shortened version of their wartime .30-06 (7.62×63mm) cartridge. This was adopted as the standard NATO rifle round in December 1953. In the interests of NATO standardization, the EM-2 project was cancelled, and Britain adopted the 7.62×51mm NATO round. It is perhaps ironic to note that within a decade, however, the US military had itself adopted an 'intermediate' cartridge, the 5.56×45mm round of the M16.

Towards the 7.62mm NATO Bren

Once Britain accepted the 7.62×51mm NATO round, it quickly adopted a version of the Belgian FN FAL rifle to fire it. The original FAL was a selective-fire rifle feeding from a 20-round box magazine, and the modified semi-automatic version adopted by the British was designated the L1A1 Self-Loading Rifle, commonly known as the SLR. A heavy-barrel 'squad automatic weapon' (SAW) version of the FN FAL rifle existed, and was briefly tested by the British as the X8 automatic rifle. The test merely confirmed the Army's opinion that this role could be done better by a re-chambered version of the Bren, however, and Britain did not buy this version of the weapon.

Odd and unusual Brens

The vast majority of Bren guns were produced in either .303in, or later in 7.62×51mm NATO. A few, however, were produced in other calibres. Most were merely one-off prototypes, but some were produced in significant quantity.

The Nationalist Chinese forces had adopted the Zb 26 before the war, and used the weapon to fight the Japanese. The Canadian Inglis factory produced a version of the Mk II Bren chambered for the same 7.92mm Mauser cartridge for supply to Chinese forces from 1944. Almost 43,000 such guns were produced, though some of the last batch of 3,700 seem not to have been delivered. They were fitted with straight magazines for the rimless Mauser rounds, interchangeable with those of the original Zb 26. When the Nationalists retreated to Taiwan after their defeat by the communists following World War II, they continued to produce a version of the Inglis Mk II Bren known as the M41, chambered for the US .30-06 (7.62×63mm) cartridge.

Some Brens were converted to the US .30-06 cartridge after World War II for use by the Italian police, which seems a rather quixotic conversion given the difficulty of converting from a shorter cartridge to a longer one and the ready availability of surplus weapons already chambered for the US calibre. Perhaps the oddest Brens, however, were some 7.92mm Inglis Brens captured from the Nationalists by the communist Chinese and converted to fire the Soviet 7.62×39mm round used by the AK-47 assault rifle, feeding from standard 30-round AK-47 magazines.

Finally, a number of Brens were modified in experiments to improve the Bren in various ways. An example was the use of Bakelite furniture to replace wood, which could warp or rot under jungle conditions, but the Bakelite proved insufficiently rugged. Even more unusual was an experimental Bren featuring a reversible barrel with a chamber at each end. The idea was that once the wear on the first chamber became excessive, the barrel could be reversed to use the unworn chamber, prolonging barrel life. However, this proved to be more trouble than it was worth, and was never adopted.

As well as reducing the need to re-train troops on a new weapon, such a Bren conversion would also be cheaper, since it would use the large existing stockpile of wartime guns. The first 7.62mm Bren conversion was designated the X10E1, and was based on a modified Mk III. Once again, breech blocks from the Canadian-made 7.92mm guns were used. Considerable internal modification was required to take the new round, but the main visible differences were the barrel and magazine. The barrel was 2in longer than the shortened barrel of the original Mk III, and terminated in a cylindrical cage-type flash hider similar to that on the L1A1 rifle, rather than the cone type used on the original Bren.

The new 30-round magazine had a significantly reduced curve compared to the original, since unlike British .303in ammunition, the 7.62×51mm NATO rounds were rimless. The X10E1 could also accept the 20-round magazine of the FN FAL; the ability to share magazines with the section's riflemen in an emergency was a feature of all the 7.62mm Brens. It was possible to do the reverse and use the 30-round Bren magazine in the rifle, but not recommended; it was designed to feed downwards, and the springs were not strong enough to reliably feed upwards against gravity.

The L4A1 (top) and L4A4 Brens. Note the much straighter magazine for the rimless 7.62mm rounds, and the SLR-type slotted (rather than cone-shaped) flash suppressors. The L4A4 also has reinforcing inserts in the magazine-well sides, which the L4A1 lacks. (Author)

The L4 series of 7.62mm NATO Brens

The X10E1 was standardized as the L4A1 Light Machine Gun, and some 1,500 guns were converted from Mk III Brens in 1955–56. Unfortunately, the L4A1 had been designed to accept the magazine of the original FN FAL, and one of the changes made between the original Belgian design and the British L1A1 SLR was a modification to make the magazine locking lug larger and stronger.

An L4A4 gunner on foot patrol in Belfast, Northern Ireland, 1975. Note the circular reinforcing inserts clearly visible below the magazine. (Royal Marines Museum Collection – Crown Copyright MOD1975)

The L4A1 was thus unable to share magazines with the SLR, one of the primary aims of the conversion. Those L4A1s that had already been converted were declared obsolete with the introduction of the L4A2 in 1958, though some remained in storage much longer. They were superseded by the L4A2, which featured a modified magazine well to accept the amended magazines used in the British SLR, as well as other changes for more reliable feeding. This came into service in 1958, and was again a conversion of the Mk III. Externally, the main differences from the L4A1 are the circular body inserts supporting the magazine lips; these can be seen on each side of the gun, immediately below the magazine. All in all, 7,600 weapons were converted. The L4A3 was very similar to the L4A2, except that it was based on Mk II guns, rather than Mk III. In practical terms, the differences between the two versions were negligible. Both were declared obsolete in 1960 when they were replaced by the L4A4, though a number of L4A3s remained in Royal Navy service.

All the above guns had been issued with two steel barrels, like the .303in Brens, but in 1961 the War Office approved the L4A4, which replaced these with a single chromed barrel. Although the chroming increased the cost of the barrel by about 12 per cent, it also meant that the barrels took significantly longer to overheat when firing, and doubled barrel life, so that a spare barrel no longer needed to be issued with these guns.

The L4A4 was introduced in 1961, with 6,900 guns being created by retrofitting the barrels of L4A2 Brens, along with 500 newly converted weapons. The L4A4 was the last standard-issue version of the Bren, and remained in service through the Falklands War of 1982 and (on a very limited scale) into the 1st Gulf War of 1990–91. In addition to its service with British forces, the L4A4 was also sold to Ghana, Libya, Rhodesia and Nigeria.

The L4A5 was a similar retrofit of a number of Mk II-based L4A3 guns still in Royal Navy service with a chromed barrel, while the L4A6 was a similar conversion of withdrawn L4A1 guns. Neither seems to have been produced in large numbers. The L4A7 was a proposed 7.62mm NATO conversion of the Mk I Bren, but this never got past the prototype stage. The L4A8 and L4A9 were both essentially modifications of the L4A4 to take night-sight brackets. None of the former appears to have actually been produced at all, and very few of the latter.

The Bren GPMG

Although the converted Bren guns described above gave good service, war experience of the German MG 34 and MG 42 meant that the British Army wanted a heavier, belt-fed weapon as its new section machine gun when it switched over to the 7.62mm NATO round. A team at Enfield produced what became known as the X11 series in an attempt to meet this requirement. Like the earlier Taden gun, they were essentially Bren guns modified for belt feed, but with a conventional pistol grip and butt, rather than the spade grips of the Taden.

The X11 series were comparatively tested against other LMGs including the X16 (another belt-fed Bren derivative, produced as a private venture by BSA), the US M60, the Belgian FN MAG, the French AA52, the Danish Madsen-Saetter and the Swiss SIG MG 55-2 and MG 55-3 in 1957. The X11 and FN MAG were judged to have done best, and both went forward for improvements and further testing. The British government decided to abandon the X11 series in 1958, however, probably because of the substantial investment in tooling and equipment that would be required to put it into production, and adopted the FN MAG as the L7A1 GPMG.

The X11 series appears to have been a competent if somewhat complex weapon, though there were issues around the belt feed; the design was driven by the recoiling piston, which produced considerable friction and meant that the feed did not always have sufficient force to lift a full belt under adverse conditions or at high elevation.

The Bren-derived X11E2 belt-fed GPMG prototype on a bipod mount. (© Royal Armouries, Pattern Room Collection)

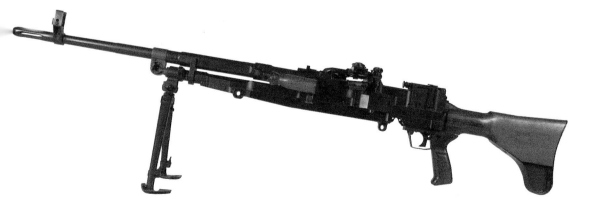

USE
The backbone of the infantry section

THE BREN IN WORLD WAR II

'The Bren L.M.G. is the principal weapon of the infantry' asserted the 'Lecture for NCOs' included in all wartime editions of the Bren manual, while rifles 'will be needed to augment the fire of the L.M.G. when required in an emergency, for local protection, and especially for "sniping" single enemy' (War Office 1942: 34). This unequivocal statement summarizes the importance placed on the Bren gun by the British Army. Every infantry section was to be built around a Bren gun, which would provide the main killing power of the section. Meanwhile, the riflemen were to serve as its ammunition bearers, provide local security, and if necessary act as replacement crew to replace casualties. Even the British 1937 Pattern Webbing worn by every rifleman, with its distinctive large twin ammunition pouches on the chest, was designed specifically to hold Bren magazines, as were the later 1944 and 1958 Patterns of Webbing.

While individual ammunition loads varied in different times and places, that set out in the 1944 edition of *Infantry Training* may serve as a typical example. It divided the section into two sub-units, the Rifle Group and the Bren Group. The seven-man rifle group was led by the section commander, usually a corporal, and consisted of:

- one NCO (Corporal) armed with a 9mm Sten gun and five magazines (150 rounds) plus two Mills bombs (No. 36 Grenades)
- six riflemen, each armed with a .303in Lee-Enfield No. 4 rifle and ten clips (50 rounds), plus two Bren magazines (60 rounds), a Mills bomb and either a shovel or a pickaxe to dig fighting positions.

The three-man Bren group was led by the section second-in-command, usually a lance-corporal, and consisted of:

- one NCO (Lance Corporal) armed with a .303in Lee-Enfield No. 4 rifle and ten clips (50 rounds), plus four Bren magazines (120 rounds) and a machete or a smatchet (a heavy-bladed knife) to clear brush
- one Bren No. 1 armed with a Bren LMG plus four Bren magazines (120 rounds) and the Bren tool wallet, containing small tools and spares for the gun
- one Bren No. 2 armed with a .303in Lee-Enfield No. 4 rifle and ten clips (50 rounds), plus five Bren magazines (150 rounds), a Mills bomb and a pickaxe, and the Bren spare-barrel carrier, containing the spare barrel, cleaning rod and other tools.

This gave each section a fairly impressive 25 Bren magazines, holding 750 rounds, plus another 250 rounds on the platoon truck. It is perhaps instructive to note that with the exception of the section leader, every man in the section carried more ammunition for the section Bren than for their own personal weapon. The No. 2 (and sometimes other members of the Bren team) carried a pair of utility pouches connected by a yoke, which were used to collect magazines from other members of the section; wherever possible, the Bren team used the magazines carried by their comrades first, and kept the magazines in their own pouches for an emergency. Unlike German machine-gunners, or British Lewis gunners during World War I, neither of the Bren numbers (crewmen) was routinely issued pistols, though they are sometimes seen carrying them in wartime photographs.

A Bren on a tripod mount during a pre-war exercise. Note that the crew are still wearing service dress and blancoed World War I-era 1908 Pattern webbing, which made no provision for carrying Bren magazines. (IWM Army Training 1938 2/20)

Anti-tank tactics (previous pages)

Canadian troops fighting off an attack by elements of 12. SS-Panzer-Division 'Hitlerjugend' shortly after D-Day. Although their rifle-calibre bullets wouldn't penetrate armour, Brens were a key part of any anti-tank plan. Their fire would force tanks to 'close up' and would suppress any accompanying infantry. With their visibility drastically reduced, tank crews became vulnerable to tank-hunter teams armed with weapons such as the PIAT (Projector, Infantry, Anti-Tank) visible here as a two-man team work their way around for a shot at the weaker side armour of this PzKpfw IV. As well as at the exposed commander, Bren gunners were taught to fire at a tank's vision blocks, and some German tanks were fitted with dummy vision blocks to draw fire away from the real ones.

In addition to the Bren in each infantry section, an infantry battalion included a carrier platoon as part of its HQ company. This included 13 Universal Carriers (generally referred to as 'Bren Gun Carriers'), in four sections of three vehicles each, plus a carrier for the platoon commander. Each of these carriers was armed with a Bren, and had a three-man crew, effectively providing a reserve of motorized Bren teams. The British Army manual on the carrier platoon reminded officers that 'Carriers should not be used as tanks and sent into action with all their guns blazing. Rather, they should be regarded as armoured mobile L.M.Gs., their mobility and armour being used to move them quickly from one fire position to another' (War Office 1943: 7).

Finally, Brens were held by other units for close defence or anti-aircraft protection. For example, each two-gun artillery section generally had a Bren for air defence, as did a proportion of logistics vehicles.

The cornerstone of rifle-section tactics

The 1937 edition of *Infantry Training*, issued a month before the first Bren gun left the factory, still shows a tactical model not much different from that of 1918. It depicts a platoon of specialized sections 'equipped primarily for fire, as light machine gun sections, or for manoeuvre, as rifle sections' (War Office 1937: 130). The next edition of the equivalent section of *Infantry Training* did not appear until March 1944, but many

British scale of issue, personal weapons, 1944

	Infantry division	Armoured division	Airborne division
Officers and men	18,347	14,964	12,416
Pistols and revolvers	1,011	2,324	2,942
Rifles	11,254	6,689	7,171
Sten guns	6,525	6,204	6,504
Bren guns	1,262	1,376	966
Vickers guns	40	22	46
PIATs	436	302	392

of the tactical changes it describes had been in place since the start of the war. Indeed, tactical practice with the Bren continued to evolve throughout the war, for example in the reduced emphasis placed on firing from a tripod.

In the attack, the section could split into two and advance by bounds, the Bren group and rifle group taking it in turns to provide cover for the other as it advanced. Equally, in a platoon-level attack, two or more complete sections could cover each other in the same manner. 'One group must always be either firing or down in a position from which fire can be instantly opened. Always have "one leg on the ground"' (War Office 1944: 55). Where possible, the two elements would form a 90-degree angle with the enemy at the apex: 'This enables the gun to give covering fire up to the last possible moment. It is of course an ideal which will not always be attained' (War Office 1944: 55).

Even though this covering fire was not expected to inflict significant casualties – 'if the enemy is dug in, covering fire seldom kills him' (War Office 1944: 53) – it should suppress the enemy, allowing the rifle group to get close enough for a final short rush to clear the position with bayonets, grenades and automatic fire from the section leader's Sten. 'Every section is designed to provide its own covering fire within itself. It can, if necessary, rely on itself to get forward. This provision of covering fire is the primary task of the Bren gun in the attack; i.e. to help get the riflemen forward' (War Office 1944: 53). When attacking a position, a good deal of stress was placed on trying to work a Bren around to the flank, and ideally positioning an additional Bren where it would be able to deliver enfilade fire on enemy troops as they fell back, having been driven out of their positions by the assault.

Obviously, not all assaults could be delivered in such a methodical manner, and one of the great advantages of the Bren was that it could be used from its sling as a one-man assault weapon, delivering heavy fire to assault a position or mount a hasty counter-attack. A good example comes from the Victoria Cross citation of Australian Leslie Starcevich. His unit, 2/43rd Australian Infantry Battalion, was moving down a track through thickly wooded ground in Borneo in June 1945 when the Japanese attacked. According to his citation, gazetted 8 November 1945:

> When the leading section came under fire from two enemy machine-gun posts and suffered casualties, Private Starcevich, who was a Bren gunner, moved forward and assaulted each post in turn. He rushed each post firing his Bren gun from the hip, killed five enemy and put the remaining occupants of the posts to flight.
>
> The advance progressed until the section came under fire from two machine gun posts which halted the section temporarily. Private Starcevich again advanced fearlessly, firing his Bren gun from the hip and ignoring the hostile fire, captured both posts single handed, disposing of seven enemy.

In defence, a great deal depended on how much time was available for preparation. Earlier versions of *Infantry Training* set out a series of steps for fortifying a position, starting with simple slit trenches and working up by stages to a fully connected trench line with alternate and fall-back positions, but the 1944 edition assumes that such complex field works are unlikely to be generally needed in a mobile war.

Bren pits were normally dug in a dogleg shape, rather than the rectangular slit trench used by a pair of riflemen, so that the No. 2 was at right angles to the gun and could adjust the gas regulator easily. Rifle and Bren pits were not generally provided with overhead cover, to allow them to engage attacking aircraft. Bren guns were to be placed at the ends of the defended section, so that they could fire along the line of attack, rather than at right angles to it, as this would place more attackers in the gun's beaten zone.

If there was time to create wire entanglements or lay mines, they needed to be covered by fire to be effective. When defending a window or loophole in a building, the Bren was to be kept well back from the opening so that its position was not obvious. Concealment was regarded as more important than fields of fire, which were often shorter than might be expected – '100 to 150 yds should suffice for both rifles and L.M.Gs.' (War Office 1944: 112) – as the intention was for the defenders to hold their fire until it would have maximum effect, rather than give away their positions by firing as soon as the enemy was in sight: 'Hold your fire until they are right close up and they should all be dead men' (War Office 1944: 21).

At night, some or all of the Brens might be set up on fixed-line tripods to cover particular danger areas, such as gaps left in the wire to allow the defenders to send out patrols. Such guns were only to fire on orders, rather than give away their position by firing on their own initiative; the Japanese, in particular, often taunted Commonwealth troops at night to provoke a response. Of course, those who fell for this often found themselves on the receiving end of sniper fire or mortars. When time permitted, tripod legs might be weighted with sandbags to make them more stable, while boards (often from 'Compo' ration crates) were sometimes put under bipod legs on soft ground, to prevent the gun digging itself in as it fired.

A South African Bren gunner uses the cover of a doorway as his section advances through Florence, Italy, August 1944. (IWM NA 17636)

A well-conducted defence could inflict very significant casualties on an advancing enemy, as this account from Sergeant James Drake of 16th Durham Light Infantry indicates. His unit was dug in outside Sedjenane, Tunisia, in early 1943:

> I had put a Bren on each flank, about fifty yards apart, so they could fire across our front in a crossfire. I gave strict instructions that nobody must fire a shot until I said so ... I waited until they had got within a hundred yards before I gave a fire order. I said 'Right, lads, fire!' Both the Brens started and we simply mowed them down. They all fell flat. The Brens kept going, and we were getting very little fire back. Some rounds splattering through the cactus trees. I says 'Right, if you see any movement in anyone, put a bullet in him ... [The battle continued throughout the day, until] ... By now, the light was fading. We'd been there since first thing that morning, and fired a lot of ammunition ... on both the Brens, the barrels were bent, including the two spares ... We had nothing more to fight them with. (Quoted in Thompson 2010: 293–94)

In a hasty defence, there might not be time to dig in, and Bren gunners might have to use the best natural cover available – hedge-lines, ditches, or folds in the ground.

Even the firepower of a single Bren could significantly slow an advancing enemy. Marine James Kelly, a Bren gunner of No. 41 (Royal

Bren tripods

Three tripods were issued for the Bren, to allow the weapon to be used in a sustained-fire role. The initial Mk 1 tripod was based on the Czech-designed tripod for the Zb 26, and could be configured as an anti-aircraft mount as well as a ground tripod. It consisted of a triangular frame with an adjustable leg at each point of the triangle, and weighed 29lb. A two-part anti-aircraft leg was stored inside the tubes forming the long sides of the triangle, one part in each. This could be removed and fixed together, then clipped to the front of the tripod to form a longer third leg, while the normal front leg pivoted upwards to form a high-angle mount for the gun. In an emergency, a Lee-Enfield rifle could be used instead of the AA leg, attaching to the tripod by the bayonet boss.

The Mk 2 tripod introduced in 1941 was significantly simpler, and omitted the features to convert it for anti-aircraft use. The Mk 2* tripod introduced in 1944 was a modification of the Mk 2 tripod for airborne use, with a folding rear quadrant to allow it to be folded into a more compact package.

ABOVE A Mk I Bren on a Mk 2 tripod. Note that the rear elevating screw of the tripod attaches to the socket originally used for the butt handle. Unlike the more complex Mk 1 tripod (which looked almost identical when set up in a ground role), the Mk 2 tripod did not convert into an anti-aircraft mount. (Author)

The initial plan was that each Bren gun would be provided with a tripod, but in practice they were not often used, and the scale of issue was dropped to five per infantry company – one per rifle platoon, plus two more with the company HQ to be handed out as needed. Rather more than half the 126,000 Bren tripods produced were made in Canada, though the Mk 2* was only made in the UK.

Marine) Commando, became separated from his unit on D-Day, 6 June 1944, and an officer from another unit pushed him into line to help stem a German counter-attack:

> He had binoculars and he was lying alongside me and it was very easy to comply with the fire control order that he gave me. A green field was stretching out in front of us and it came to a little hedgerow and a wooded area beyond it. 'They're all along that hedgerow' he says. So all I had to use was the edge of the field and the bottom of the hedgerow as my aiming mark and it was quite easy to take aim at. So I opened up with a few long bursts.

Ammunition

The Bren used British .303in ammunition (7.7×56mm). This was originally adopted in 1888 as a black-powder-filled round with a round-nosed bullet, but had gone through a number of improvements. By the time that the Mk VII version was introduced in 1910 the .303 used a more powerful smokeless cordite propellant and had a ballistically superior pointed bullet, and the Mk VII continued in use until the round was replaced in service in the 1950s. Its rimmed design was perfectly adequate for bolt-action rifles or the belt-fed Vickers gun, but as we have seen, it was not ideal for magazine-fed automatic weapons such as the Bren. According to War Office figures, at 200yd the 174-grain (0.4oz or 11.3g) bullet would penetrate 58in of softwood, 18in of well-packed sandbags, or 14in of brick. Anyone unfortunate enough to be hit by such a bullet 'went down, and stayed down' as one officer put it.

ABOVE Each Bren section was issued two rigid magazine boxes, each holding 12 magazines in metal clips. Although magazines were generally split out among the section members, the boxes provided extra protection in transit, and were sometimes seen in the front line, particularly when the section was on the defensive. (Author)

The more powerful Mk VIII ammunition, with a slightly heavier boat-tailed bullet and more powerful propellant charge, was intended to achieve maximum range from the Vickers MMG. It was not supposed to be used in rifles or Brens except in emergencies, as it caused significant barrel erosion in these weapons.

The rimless 7.62×51mm NATO round used in re-chambered Brens was 5mm (0.2in) shorter than the .303in but its muzzle velocity was only slightly lower with a bullet of the same weight, since the .303in cartridge case (originally designed for black powder) did not make the most efficient use of modern propellant.

Tracer was used against aircraft when available, but not generally against ground targets except on exercises. This was partly because while the belts for Vickers guns came factory loaded with 1-in-5 tracer, Bren magazines were usually filled in the field from the same boxes of .303in ball as the section's rifles. It was also partly because while tracer rounds let the

gunner see where his rounds were going, they also made his own position very obvious.

Although the Bren magazine theoretically held 30 rounds, it was normal practice to only load 28 or so; this reduced the magazine-spring pressure, and let the rounds feed more reliably. There were several proposals to pre-package Bren ammunition in disposable 14-round chargers, to allow faster reloading of magazines in the field. Trial versions of the chargers worked well, but the idea was never taken up as the Bren chargers could not be used to load rifles, complicating ammunition supply.

Loss and damage to magazines was a perennial problem, and there were various proposals to produce factory-loaded 'expendable' magazines for both the Bren and Sten. However, all foundered on the difficulties of producing something reliable and robust enough to stand up to field use and still cheap enough to be thrown away after use.

One of the neatly drawn illustrations from the 1939 Bren manual, showing the grip initially taught, with the left hand below the butt. This was found to be insufficiently stable, and amended to the grip shown in the photo opposite. (1939 manual, page 12)

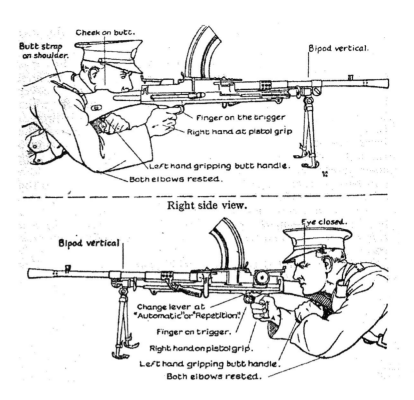

You could see clumps of them moving about and I kept firing. Then it died down and I switched the gun to single rounds, which was the drill to do. You fired bursts when you had a good target to shoot at but the Bren was always used to confuse the enemy – that was what we were taught – so that the enemy wouldn't know if it was a machine gun firing at them or a rifle. So you switched to single shots when you could and when I did it on this occasion it was just like being on the firing point in practice …

I think I was the only one who had a really clear field of fire so he kept supplying me with ammunition and loading the magazines for me and I kept up this steady rate of fire. But of course the Germans don't take that lying down – if they've got a troublesome point they try to eliminate it as much as we would – so it wasn't very long before I was getting mortared then and I realised I was the target. They came fairly close but I didn't take much notice of them except on one occasion when the burst was really close …

This went on for some time until:

It must have been late afternoon, we must have been in this battle right through the day, I didn't know it was going to end but the order must have come through 'Well, OK, you can pull out now'. I got told 'keep up a steady rate of fire now because we're running down the ammo'….

Kelly and the officer fell back, Kelly noting wryly: 'We were running through an orchard towards a big wall at the end and even though I was

A Canadian gunner showing the firing grip taught later, with the hand on the neck of the butt. This had replaced the previous grip well before the 1942 manual was printed. (IWM NA 11564)

encumbered by the Bren gun I still made the wall before he did' (Quoted in Bailey 2009: 347–52).

Learning to use the Bren

Machine-gunners in World War I had been specialists, and the majority of infantrymen were not trained to use one. This was to change with the adoption of the Bren, and all wartime editions of the Bren manual state that 'The light machine gun is the principal weapon of the infantry and every man will, therefore, be trained to use it' (War Office 1939: 47). Given the relatively straightforward operation of the Bren, this was much easier to achieve than would have been the case with its much more complex predecessors, the Vickers and Lewis guns, both of which required considerable specialist training to use.

The Bren manual itself was structured as a series of lesson plans, covering the tactical use of the gun and selecting suitable positions as well as firing and maintaining the weapon. All infantrymen learned the basics of using the Bren, including live firing, during their initial recruit training. As a rule, only those actually assigned as No. 1 or No. 2 on the gun were taught the less common aspects, such as mounting the weapon on the tripod to cover fixed lines, and only they received the Bren gun proficiency badge worn on the sleeve of the battledress. That said, other men might have to take over the gun to replace casualties, and not every man carrying a Bren always had the proficiency badge, especially in units that had been in combat for some time.

Training in non-infantry units varied; armoured or artillery units often had Brens for anti-aircraft use, but not all their men were necessarily trained to use them. Lieutenant D'Arcy McCloughlin of the Royal Engineers, looking back on the retreat to Dunkirk, lamented: 'We had had quite insufficient practice. The idea of shooting from a Bren, using tracer

Firing the Bren

To load the Bren, the gunner (or No. 2) slid open the magazine-well cover, placed the front edge of the magazine under the lip of the magazine well, and pulled the body of the magazine back until it locked in place. Magazines held 30 rounds in theory, but the rimmed .303in rounds did not always feed well, and the later editions of the manual recommended only loading 28 rounds per magazine. It was very important to ensure that the cartridges were not loaded into the magazine 'rim behind rim', as this would cause a stoppage. Once the magazine was in place, the gunner reached forward and pulled back the cocking handle to chamber the first round.

The Bren's top-mounted magazine meant that sights were offset

ABOVE An Australian Bren gunner firing at Japanese positions on Bougainville, Papua New Guinea, April 1945. He has fastened the tool wallet (usually carried on the webbing) to the butt of his Bren. (AWM 091023)

to the left side of the weapon; there was no sensible way to fire the weapon from the left shoulder as one could with a rifle. Sights were adjusted for range by rotating the drum of the back sight (Mk I Bren) or by sliding the adjuster on the ladder-type back sight (later versions) until it corresponded to the gunner's estimate of range to target. If time allowed when defending fixed positions, ranges might be paced out and marked with piles of stones. (Sights need

and taking on low-flying aircraft, had never occurred to anyone and none of us had been trained in it' (Quoted in Levine 2010: 45).

Since repeated stripping and reassembly, cocking and dry-firing led to wear and poor fit of the working parts of the gun, old and worn-out guns were deactivated and converted into 'Drill Purpose' guns for recruit training, clearly marked as 'DP' in white paint. The 1942 edition of the manual also found it necessary to urge stripping and reassembly be limited to that necessary for cleaning, and to prohibit practising stripping and assembly 'against the clock', though this prohibition was not always obeyed.

Of course, men did not always remember their training perfectly amid the adrenalin of combat. Lieutenant Tony Pawson of 10th Rifle Brigade recalls ambushing a German motorcycle and side-car in Tunisia in early 1943:

> I had a Bren gun. Instead of lying down and firing in short bursts, I was so excited I fired the whole magazine standing up from the hip. I planned to fire at the motorcycle to prevent it getting away, but missed. One of the Germans had a go at me. I was stupidly still standing up.

to be adjusted because gravity and air resistance mean that bullets actually travel in a parabola, rather than a straight line. Adjusting the sights changes the point of aim to compensate for this.)

The Bren had a three-position safety catch, marked 'S' (Safe), 'R' (for 'Rounds', i.e. semi-automatic) and 'A' (for full-automatic fire). The single-shot 'R' setting was used to allow the Bren to fire without giving away the presence of a machine gun until the enemy were within good killing range. However, the normal practice in combat was to use 4–5-round bursts; shorter bursts made it difficult to observe the impact of rounds, while longer bursts wasted ammunition and overheated the barrel too quickly.

Cartridge cases were ejected downwards, which was generally a positive feature in an infantry gun; the flicker of cases ejected upwards or sideways from weapons such as the Lewis gun drew the eye, and could give away the gunner's position. It was less advantageous in a vehicle pintle mount, where the ejected cartridges rained down on the rest of the crew. Drivers of Daimler Dingo scout cars seemed particularly likely to receive red-hot spent shell cases down the back of the neck, and several commented to the effect that this could be something of a distraction! A canvas bag to catch spent cases was designed, but not always issued or used.

Recoil was not too bad, and generally less than the Lee-Enfield rifle, because of the weight of the gun and because the gas system tapped off some of the energy. However, the manual emphasized the importance of a good firm grip, especially when firing from the hip.

The gunner could easily develop a kind of 'tunnel vision', focusing on the limited field of view visible through the sights and the No. 2 was fully occupied keeping the gun supplied with fresh magazines or reloading empty magazines from bandoliers of loose rounds. It was therefore the job of the lance-corporal commanding the Bren team to spot new targets for the gun to engage, and keep abreast of the flow of battle to recognize when the team should move forward to a new position or fall back.

After firing ten magazines at the 'Rapid Rate' of four magazines per minute, the barrel would start to overheat and need changing. This would normally be done by the No. 2, by disengaging the barrel-nut catch, rotating the barrel nut and pushing forward the carrying handle to remove the barrel. The spare barrel carried by the No. 2 would then be locked into place, and the gun could continue firing while the original barrel was laid aside to cool. If there was a stream or puddle nearby, the hot barrel would be laid in this; even wet grass significantly helped to cool the barrel.

This quick and easy barrel change was one of the great strengths of the Bren. A well-trained crew could change barrels in 6–8 seconds, and maintain sustained fire almost without interruption, a very significant advantage over fixed-barrel weapons like the US BAR. The well-designed carrying handle fitted to the barrel of the Bren also had the enormous advantage that the No. 2 could handle the hot barrel without any special precautions to avoid burning his hands, an almost unique feature on guns of the period. For example, barrel changes on the German MG 34 and MG 42 series required the gunner to use a thick and clumsy felt pad to hold the hot barrel, while even the postwar US M60 needed the gunner to use an asbestos glove for barrel changes.

Despite all my Bren gun training I couldn't understand why it wasn't firing – of course the magazine was empty and I hadn't got another magazine handy. (Quoted in Thompson 2010: 277–78)

Other men went to the opposite extreme, focusing on the drills they had practised no matter what was going on around them. Sergeant James Bellows of 1st Royal Hampshire remembered that on D-Day:

I witnessed something that you only expect to see in training. These two men were firing with their Bren gun ... the gun jammed. They both slithered to the bottom of the hole they were in. With a Bren gun you've got a wallet with various parts and various tools for various stoppages, and they opened the wallet, as on par for parade, took out their tools, stripped their gun, cleared their fault, put it back together again, closed the wallet, even put the little straps through their brass links, then went back up the hill and carried on firing. (Quoted in Bailey 2009: 319)

Most men, of course, fell somewhere between the two extremes.

Two members of the Home Guard with a Bren and a Thompson SMG, in December 1940. A Home Guard unit would be very lucky indeed to receive a Bren rather than a Lewis or BAR; one cannot help suspecting that the Bren has been 'loaned' for this propaganda shoot. (IWM H 5839)

Blitzkrieg and Home Defence 1939–40

The Bren was a relatively new and recently adopted weapon when war broke out in 1939, and the British Army had not yet fully re-equipped. As it was, almost every available Bren went to France with the BEF. These guns saw heavy use against the attacking German forces initially. Once the Allied front had collapsed, however, and the retreating British units were ordered to abandon and burn their vehicles, many Brens were left behind along with other heavy equipment. Some units did retain their Brens during the retreat to Dunkirk, but most were more concerned with avoiding German troops and carrying wounded comrades, and did not. Units that had experienced fouling problems (often made worse by lack of cleaning during the chaotic conditions of the retreat) were particularly likely to abandon their Brens. Some were even destroyed unissued, as the BEF blew up or burnt its supply dumps as it retreated.

When the Army took stock after the evacuation, it discovered that there were only 2,300 Bren guns in the country, only enough to equip about two divisions. A plan was immediately put into place to increase production of the Bren by simplifying it, and a contingency plan developed for a simple-to-produce LMG (the Besal) as a stopgap in case of invasion, but both of these would take time to bear fruit. In the meantime, the government issued thousands of old obsolete Lewis guns (often the aircraft version, without the distinctive aluminium barrel shroud) and

Brens for the French Resistance

The Bren's light weight and the fact that it could be carried by a single man made it ideal for the French Resistance, and relatively large numbers were supplied by air drop. Very approximately, one in ten of the weapons supplied to the Resistance during the war were Brens, with the remainder being split roughly evenly between rifles and SMGs, plus a small number of pistols and anti-tank weapons such as the American Bazooka and British PIAT (Projector, Infantry, Anti-Tank).

Some arms were dropped to other Resistance movements such as the various Yugoslav partisan groups, but simple distance restricted this until airfields in Italy and the Mediterranean became available, and in many cases, the RAF's Bomber Command saw arms drops as an unwelcome distraction from what it regarded as its primary mission – bombing Germany's productive capacity to rubble.

Bizarrely, some of the 7.92mm Brens of the type made by Inglis for the Nationalist Chinese, but without the Chinese markings, were apparently passed to the British Special Operations Executive (SOE). The idea was presumably that since they used the standard German rifle round, Resistance groups equipped with them would be able to use captured ammunition. However, this would equally have meant that they couldn't use other ammunition supplies provided by SOE,

ABOVE A member of the French Forces of the Interior with a British-supplied Bren, Châteaudun, France, 1944. (Cody Images)

which would seem to outweigh this, and it is not clear how many, if any, of these guns were actually dropped into Occupied Europe.

purchased 25,000 Browning Automatic Rifles and 40,000 Lewis guns from the United States. Both the latter were surplus US Army weapons chambered for the US .30-06 cartridge, rather than the .303in conversion of the BAR tested at the same time as the Bren or the World War I British .303in version of the Lewis. Almost all of these weapons went to the Home Guard, which at least meant that all of the Brens produced could be issued to the Army.

The Middle East and North Africa 1941–43

Since the BEF in France had received first priority for the issue of the new Brens, British units in the Middle East had generally not been issued with the newer guns when the war broke out, and were often still soldiering on with rather elderly Lewis guns. Shortages of the Bren continued into the fighting in the Western Desert in 1941–42; most British units had their full complement of Bren guns, but Indian Army units (including their British battalions) were still equipped with the serviceable but inferior Vickers-Berthier, while Captain Vernon Northwood, an officer serving with 2/28th Australian Infantry Battalion, 9th Australian Division, talks of having to use captured Italian Breda LMGs (Thompson 2010: 36). Photographs of vehicles (especially Long Range Desert Group trucks) from this period often show a variety of machine guns such as the Vickers K, scrounged from a variety of sources including wrecked aircraft.

A Bren gunner in North Africa, June 1943. Using the 100-round AA drum in the ground role like this was unusual, as it blocked the normal sights. One suspects it is simple posing for the camera, rather than a real intention to use the weapon like this. (IWM NA 3345)

Lend-Lease Brens

The Red Army probably do not immediately leap to mind as users of the Bren gun, and Western readers are generally used to thinking of Lend-Lease aid as something Britain received, rather than something that Britain provided to other countries. However, after the invasion of the Soviet Union in 1941, Britain dispatched whatever aid could be spared via convoys to the Arctic port of Murmansk. This included everything from food and medical supplies to fighter aircraft, although it did not include significant quantities of small arms since the Soviets could produce enough of these themselves. It did, however, include roughly 7,000 Universal Carriers, Valentine and Matilda tanks. Each vehicle was shipped with full stowed equipment, including a Bren gun per vehicle. These guns were often passed on as infantry weapons if the vehicle itself was disabled or worn out.

For propaganda reasons, the Soviets were reluctant to admit that they needed aid from countries they despised for ideological reasons, and such equipment was rarely referred to in official Soviet histories, though photographs do survive.

The desert was a challenging environment for any weapon, with its heat and constant sand and grit. Weapons could not be oiled after cleaning, as the ever-present dust quickly turned any lubricant left on the gun into a gritty paste that wore away working parts. Fortunately, the Bren had been designed with the mud of World War I trenches in mind, and apertures where dust could get into the mechanism were minimized; there was even a sliding cover to close off the magazine well when no magazine was fitted. This was a significant improvement on the Lewis gun, where the open bottoms of the pan magazines meant the cartridges tended to pick up grit, which they then carried into the weapon's mechanism. As a result, though careful cleaning was needed, there were no serious reliability problems with the Bren.

By the end of 1942, increased production in Britain, Canada and Australia meant that the shortages had disappeared, and many Indian Army units in North Africa found themselves receiving Brens to replace Vickers-Berthiers lost in combat. Most welcomed it as an improvement, since it was lighter and easier to carry. By the Tunisian campaign of 1943, almost all units were equipped with Brens, though other weapons were still occasionally seen.

The Far East 1941–45

Meanwhile, troops in the Far East had also enjoyed a relatively low priority for the newest weapons up to 1940, despite repeated requests. In fairness, the weapons were in limited supply, and it is difficult to fault the British government for giving priority to theatres where fighting was actually taking place.

The Japanese invasion of Malaya and Burma in late 1941 resulted in sweeping victories against relatively ill-prepared British and Indian Army units, and in more lost equipment and weapons. By the end of the retreat from Burma, 17th Indian Infantry Division had only 56 functioning Bren

guns left, for example, compared to the thousand-plus it should have had according to tables of equipment.

As the Japanese pushed in on the borders of British India, the forces fighting them were largely equipped with Indian-manufactured Vickers-Berthiers. More and more Brens arrived from Britain, however, both with newly arrived units and as replacements for weapons lost or worn out in the fighting. In 1942, the factory at Ishapore switched over from producing Vickers-Berthiers to producing Brens, and the latter weapon slowly came to predominate in the Far East theatre, too.

The Bren's portability was particularly well-suited to the Far East theatre, where jungle and swamp terrain meant that much of the fighting relied on what the infantry could carry themselves, and its powerful rounds penetrated vegetation cover better than the smaller-calibre rounds used by the Japanese. The Australians in particular took to the Bren, boosting numbers deployed and often using it from its sling as they advanced, so that it operated almost as a heavy automatic rifle rather than a machine gun.

An Australian Bren gunner accepts a cigarette from an American after their forces in New Guinea linked up in February 1944. The sling has been shortened to hold the gun by the hip, ready for immediate use. (AWM 070318)

Western Europe 1943–45

When the Allied invasion of Occupied Europe finally came – first through the misnamed 'soft underbelly' of Italy in 1943, and then via Normandy on D-Day, 6 June 1944 – the Bren was once again in the forefront. As well as its primary role as a section gun, it was also the primary British light AA weapon, and served as a pintle-mount weapon on a wide variety of armoured vehicles.

A Sikh Bren gunner from an Indian unit of Eighth Army in Italy, December 1943. Note the use of paint to camouflage the Bren's highly visible upright magazine. (IWM NA 9787)

The excellent sustained-fire capability of the Bren, rapidly deployed and available down to section level, was a key factor in maintaining the firepower of British infantry units, which were still equipped with bolt-action rifles at a time when their American equivalents now had semi-automatic Garand rifles, and their German opponents were increasingly equipped with the first selective-fire assault rifles.

Another advantage of the Bren became apparent in the bitter winter of 1944/45, when Commonwealth soldiers found that their Bren guns remained operational even when the water in the cooling jackets of their heavier Vickers guns froze solid.

49

AFTER WORLD WAR II

National Service 1947–60

Once the war was over, the costs of rebuilding a country damaged by bombing and worn out by six years of war meant that there was little money available for new weapons; even basic foods were still rationed into the early 1950s. This was particularly the case for the Bren, which was felt to have performed relatively effectively in its role, and was well-regarded by the troops.

The Bren's relative simplicity was a significant advantage during the National Service era, as the majority of British troops during this period were conscripts, serving for relatively short two-year enlistments. As well as the Korean War, these young conscripts took part in a number of smaller 'end of empire' military operations, including the Malayan Emergency (1948–50), the Mau Mau Uprising in Kenya (1952–60), the Suez Crisis of 1956 and the Cyprus Emergency of 1956–60. The last National Servicemen were enlisted in December 1960.

Learning to use the Bren was a common memory of National Servicemen in the Army; a lecture on the weapon even forms part of the comedy *Carry On Sergeant*, the first in a series of films which became a minor British institution of the period themselves.

A Bren gunner scans the Korean hillside opposite his dugout, early 1952. The box by his side holds 12 Bren magazines. Note the offset handle that allowed two boxes to be carried back-to-back in the same hand. (AWM LEEJ0229)

Korea 1950–53

The Japanese had ruled the Korean peninsula since before World War II, and with their defeat, it had been divided between US and Soviet occupation forces along the 38th Parallel. This quickly became a political border as well as an administrative one, with a communist regime installed in the north. North Korean troops invaded the South in June 1950, in the first major incidents in the Cold War. Their initial successes against the unprepared defending forces were quickly reversed, but when the North Koreans were driven back across the 38th Parallel, the communist People's Republic of China intervened on the North Korean side, and the United Nations forces were forced back in turn. The ferocious defence of the Imjin River line by the British 29th Infantry Brigade managed to halt the Chinese offensive, however, and the war bogged down into positional fighting.

The British troops deployed as part of the UN-sponsored 'Free World Forces' were still largely equipped with World War II-era personal weapons, though now supported by jet aircraft and Centurion tanks. In fairness, their communist opponents were in the same position, being armed largely with Soviet small arms of the same vintage. Once again, the Bren performed well, with the main difficulty being keeping the weapons operational in the bitter sub-zero conditions of the Korean winter. Instructions were issued to keep the weapons free of snow, which could build up to form ice and jam the weapons. In extremely low temperatures, gun oil froze, and Bren guns were to be cleaned with petrol to remove all traces of it, then reassembled 'dry'.

A Bren group of Princess Patricia's Canadian Light Infantry, Korea, January 1951. (Cody Images)

As an indication of how important Brens were to British units, Chinese troops fighting against them were told to identify Bren gunners and concentrate fire on them whenever possible, since taking the Bren out of action would seriously reduce the British section's firepower. During 1st Gloucestershire Regiment's stand on the Imjin River, for example, so many Brens had been damaged by incoming fire that Regimental Sergeant-Major Jack Hobbs was forced to dismantle damaged Bren guns in order to assemble working weapons from the undamaged parts of each (Salmon 2009: 203). In response, some British units tried to camouflage the Bren's distinctive upright magazine with paint or sacking, to little avail.

Ironically, some British units found themselves capturing examples of Brens supplied to the Chinese Nationalist forces for use against the Japanese during World War II, and now being used by the communists who had defeated the Nationalists.

An Australian Bren gunner waiting to go out on patrol in Korea, May 1953. He has stuffed spare magazines into his pockets, rather than wearing webbing. (AWM HOBJ4271)

Replacement by the GPMG

By the early 1950s, the World War II-era personal weapons of the British were looking decidedly out of date. The Bren was still relatively well-regarded, however, and it was entirely possible that a re-chambered version might have soldiered on as the section LMG alongside riflemen carrying the radical bullpup EM-2, and with the Bren-derived Taden gun in the sustained-fire role.

In fact, American pressure led to the adoption in 1954 of the 7.62mm NATO cartridge, and a version of the Belgian FN FAL, known as the L1A1 Self-Loading Rifle in British service. However, this was far from the end of the line for the Bren. Re-chambering existing weapons for the new calibre was relatively straightforward, and the resulting guns were even able to use the same magazines as the SLR in an emergency. Even the 1958 Pattern Webbing designed to carry magazines for the new rifle was still capable of taking the magazines of the re-chambered Brens.[3]

The Army, however, wanted a true all-round machine gun – something along the lines of the German MG 42 – which would be able to fulfil all machine-gun roles, including those such as the vehicle co-axial role that the Bren did not fill particularly well. The specification for the replacement gun obviously owed a great deal to experience with the Bren, such as the requirement for a quick barrel change without the need for special pads or gauntlets to handle the hot barrel. However, it also included a requirement for belt feed, from a disintegrating link belt of the sort used on the new US M60 machine gun.[4]

The Royal Ordnance factory at Enfield submitted a Bren-derived belt-fed weapon – the X11 gun – as a response to this specification. Competitive tests compared this with another belt-fed Bren derivative from BSA (the X16), the US M60, the Belgian FN MAG, the French AA52, the Danish Madsen-Setter and the Swiss SIG MG 55-2 and MG 55-3. The FN MAG was considered to have done best, while X11 came second. After further tests, the FN MAG was adopted as the L7A1 GPMG in 1958.

It might perhaps have been comforting to the Royal Ordnance team to know that the last descendant of the Bren had been beaten only by a truly world-class gun; at the time of writing, the L7A1 is still in front-line service with the British Army, having served well in all theatres for 55 years without significant changes. It is also in use with dozens of other armies and is currently being adopted by the US Army as the M240, an astonishing achievement for a 60-year-old weapon.

Unlike both the Canadian and Australian forces, the British Army did not buy any of the heavy-barrel SAW version of the FN FAL. It was felt that it was too light for the role and would not be able to maintain any real volume of sustained fire, an assessment that proved true when

---

3   The ammunition pouches of '58 Pattern Webbing were a little deep for standard 20-round SLR magazines. To enable them to be reached more easily, it was common practice for troops to put extra field dressings into the bottom of the pouches, to raise the magazines for easier access.

4   A disintegrating link belt is made up of stamped sheet metal links, each holding one round and attaching to the link on either side of it. The mechanism of the gun separates and ejects the links as ammunition feeds into the gun. While more complex than the webbing belts used on older guns such as the Vickers, the metal disintegrating link belts do not absorb water and freeze, and the gunner is not hampered by lengths of expended belt hanging out of his weapon.

Royal Marines in Aden, 1962. The 7.62×51mm version of the Bren served alongside the newly introduced L1A1 SLR until replaced by the belt-fed GPMG. (Royal Marines Museum Collection – Crown Copyright MOD 1962)

the weapons saw combat. Instead, the British chose to retain the re-chambered Bren in a limited number of roles, designated as 'Light Machine Gun' as opposed to the L7 'General Purpose Machine Gun'.

The Indonesian Confrontation 1963–66

As part of Britain's withdrawal from empire, the British colonies of Malaya and British Borneo were merged to form the Federation of Malaysia in 1963. However, the Indonesian government under the Nationalist President Sukarno hoped that if those territories could be destabilized, they could be merged into the Indonesian south of the island, or at least detached from British influence and converted into client states. Indonesian irregular forces began infiltrating across the long jungle border between the two countries to attack targets such as police stations. Regular Indonesian troops followed, as the situation worsened.

The first British troops involved were armed with the relatively new SLRs and Bren guns (in 7.62mm NATO), as the new L7A1 GPMG was not yet available in sufficient numbers, although this would change as the campaign progressed. Interestingly, many of the units involved believed

The Falklands, 1982 (opposite)

The Bren's last significant combat use was in the Falklands. The Royal Marines had retained a number of L4A4 versions, re-chambered for the 7.62×51mm NATO round, and deployed these to augment the firepower of their rifle sections' GPMGs. Here we see men from 42 Commando assaulting the dug-in Argentine positions on Mount Harriet, as the British forces close on Port Stanley. During the heavy fighting, the L4A4's ability to use magazines from both British SLRs and Argentine FN FAL rifles proved very useful, as the gunners were able to continue firing even after they had used up their initial ammunition loads, without calling on the limited amount of spare belted ammunition carried for the GPMGs.

that Brens were better weapons for these jungle operations, and continued to use them even once sufficient GPMGs were available. The main drawback of the GPMG was that the belted ammunition could tangle on vegetation, or could give away a patrol's position when the bullets clinked against each other or caught the light.

The Bren was also lighter, and could be fired more easily from the hip, allowing it to get into action more quickly. This was a key advantage in short-range jungle encounters that characterized the confrontation, and where the GPMG's primary advantage of better sustained fire was rarely relevant.

The ongoing Cold War

Although generally replaced by the L7A1 GPMG, the L4A4 version of the Bren continued in use in a limited range of applications. They were commonly seen in photographs of Royal Marines deployed to Norway during annual exercises to secure NATO's northern flank, often camouflaged with white tape to break up the weapon's outline, especially the prominent vertical magazine. The Royal Marines found that the enclosed magazines of the L4A4 fed more reliably in Arctic conditions than the ammunition belts of the GPMG; these tended to pick up snow, which then froze the belt solid.

The L4A4 also remained in service as a pintle-mount weapon on vehicles such as the FV 433 Abbot 105mm self-propelled gun, though in practice such weapons were rarely mounted on the vehicles they were theoretically assigned to. One soldier serving in a field-artillery regiment in 1978 commented: 'On occasion, these guns would be let out of the armoury for us to look at. On even rarer occasions they were taken on exercise' (Khan 2009: 52). It turned out that he was the only man in the troop who knew how to strip the weapon, and that was only because he had been trained on one as a cadet before joining the Army.

Royal Marines during a deployment to Northern Norway in January 1980. Note the use of white tape to break up the outline of the L4A4 and SLR. (Royal Marines Museum Collection – Crown Copyright MOD1980)

Royal Marines of No. 42 Commando in Port Stanley, June 1982. The front man carries an L4A4 while the rear man carries an L7A1 GPMG, the weapon that replaced the Bren in general service. (Royal Marines Museum Collection – Crown Copyright MOD1982)

The Falklands War 1982

The Argentinian Junta launched an invasion of the Falkland Islands (a British territory in the South Atlantic) in 1982, at least partially to use the ensuing patriotic fervour as a distraction from their country's ongoing economic problems and the regime's human-rights abuses. They had gambled that Britain would be unable to mount a counter-invasion over such a long distance. While this proved to be a miscalculation, it was very obvious to the commanders of the British Task Force dispatched to liberate the islands that the logistics of an amphibious operation 8,000 miles from home would mean that the infantry units involved would have little of the support they would have expected in the European war they had trained for.

The Royal Marines in particular therefore opted to beef up the firepower of their infantry sections by issuing each with an L4A4 light machine gun in addition to the GPMG it would usually have. The Parachute Regiment also felt that more supporting fire would be required,

Bren accessories

A large number of accessories were issued for the Bren at various points, but the most important and commonly encountered are described here. Each Bren team was issued a Bren Wallet and Bren Holdall. Patterns varied slightly between manufacturers and through time, but all were basically similar.

The Bren Wallet was a folding canvas roll carried by the No. 1 on his webbing, and contained: a combination tool to disassemble the gun; a pull-through to oil the barrel; an oil can to lubricate the gun; and a spare-parts tin holding common spares, for example a spare return spring.

The Bren Holdall was carried on a shoulder sling by the No. 2, and was commonly called the 'spare barrel carrier' since the main compartment held the spare barrel and cylinder-cleaning rod. Another pocket held the Bren Wallet described above when not in use. Other pockets carried: a bottle of 'cold weather' oil; an oil bottle of graphited grease; a mop, wire brush and magazine brush for attachment to the cylinder rod; and a fouling tool. In combat, the No. 2 often left the holdall with the unit transport, and carried just the spare barrel tucked under the flap of the pack.

Other commonly issued items were rigid magazine boxes, each holding 12 30-round .303in magazines in individual clips. Magazines were kept in them at any time when the unit was not in combat, which prevented damage to the feed lips of the magazines as they knocked around in web pouches. The handles of these magazine boxes were offset to one edge, so a pair could be carried easily in one hand by holding them back-to-back so both handles were together. An almost identical box was produced for 7.62mm NATO magazines; the original boxes could not be used with the new magazines, as they were much less sharply curved. As a consequence, the box for 7.62mm magazines

ABOVE A Bren gunner of The Royal Sussex Regiment in Burma, November 1944. He is carrying his spare magazines in what appears to be a '37-Pattern binoculars pouch, unfastened for easy access. The rectangular pouch behind his hip is the Bren's tool wallet. (IWM SE 729)

was much shallower than the .303in version. A magazine filler tool was theoretically issued, though they were not always available. Magazines could be filled without it, but it speeded up the laborious task of filling the large number needed in combat. Finally, a sturdy wooden packing case with rope handles ('Chest, Bren') was used to store and ship the weapon itself.

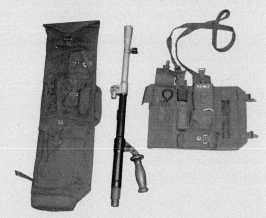

ABOVE The Bren Holdall (left) with the spare barrel, and the tool wallet (right) unrolled to show the contents, including the cleaning rod, spare-parts tin, combination tool, pull-through to clean the barrel and a rectangular oil bottle respectively. The tool wallet secured with webbing tabs when rolled, and was worn on the No. 1's webbing in action, or carried in the large external pocket of the holdall when out of the line. (Author)

but appears to have obtained additional GPMGs instead. In the case of the Royal Marines, since the other members of the section were already carrying ammunition for the section GPMG, extra rations and mortar ammunition, there was little possibility of them carrying additional magazines for the LMG on the long cross-country 'yomps' that characterized the war. Most L4A4 gunners, therefore, had only a dozen or so magazines for the gun, split between themselves and their No. 2, though they could also use magazines from other riflemen in their section.

They could (and did) also use captured Argentine magazines – by a happy coincidence, the change to a larger magazine-locking lug design made as part of the changes between the original FN FAL and the British SLR meant that British soldiers could use Argentine FN FAL magazines in their SLRs, but Argentine FALs could not use British magazines. Given that each section already had a GPMG, and ammunition for the LMGs was limited, the L4A4s were mostly used as heavy automatic rifles, rather than as section light machine guns proper.

The twilight of the Bren

The change from the 7.62mm SLR to the 5.56mm L85 (SA-80) assault rifle in the mid- to late 1980s marked the effective end of the Bren's long career with the British Army. It could no longer use the same ammunition as the rest of the infantry section, and would no longer be needed as each infantry section now had two L86 Light Support Weapons (LSW). The LSW was a version of the L85 with a longer, heavier barrel and a bipod, and was expected to be able to perform the same role as the ageing L4A4, at a lower weight.

In fact, the L86 proved inadequate in the light-support role, perhaps unsurprisingly since suggestions that it should have a quick-change barrel and fire from an open bolt to aid cooling had both been rejected since they would reduce commonality with the baseline L85 rifle, a major selling point of the design. The L86 LSW was therefore partly replaced by the FN Minimi, a more conventional 5.56mm SAW already in service with the US Army, although some were retained in the rifle squad to provide accurate semi-automatic fire or short bursts of full-automatic fire at extended ranges.

A few Brens soldiered on through the 1st Gulf War in 1990–91, as pintle-mount weapons on a few second-echelon vehicles. However, the author has not been able to find evidence that any of these weapons were actually used in action. They were largely withdrawn from service during the rationalization of equipment following the war, though the last example was not withdrawn from a Territorial Army unit until February 1999.

The very last British Brens served in Army Cadet detachments, who used both .303in and 7.62mm versions. Most of these were withdrawn in the early 1990s, to be replaced by versions of the L86 LSW. The final two guns were not handed over to the Small Arms School Collection at Warminster, however, until February 2002, 64 years after the first gun was issued.

Twin Motley AA mount fitted in the back of a light truck at the Southern Command training school in Devon, 1942. The guns are fitted with 100-round AA drums, and the little-used bags to catch ejected cases are mounted underneath. (IWM H 23073)

OTHER ROLES FOR THE BREN

The Bren in the anti-aircraft role

Providing light anti-aircraft (AA) fire had been part of the original specification of the Bren gun.[5] The Mk 1 tripod could be set up for AA work, and there were a number of specially designed AA mounts for vehicles, such as the Motley and Lakeman mounts.

A special 100-round drum (based on the drum magazine originally developed for the Vickers gas-operated aircraft gun) was issued for AA use, along with special clip-on AA sights. The magazine cover had to be replaced with a special bracket to mount the drum magazine, but this was a simple task. The drum was rather clumsy, and could not be used easily in the ground role, since it blocked the view through the gun's normal sights. AA drums were only normally issued (in wooden boxes of four drums) to guns intended primarily for AA use, and very few infantry Bren gunners even saw one. Two slightly different patterns existed, the earlier of which had a separate winding handle, while this was built into the drum in the later pattern.

5   Technically, the British Army considered 'light' anti-aircraft weapons to be the 20mm Oerlikon and Polsten cannon, and the 40mm Bofors gun, as distinct from the 'heavy' anti-aircraft guns of 3.7in or larger. However, in practice the Bren was commonly termed 'light AA' even if it didn't meet the technical definition.

A second AA drum, the Vesely High Speed Drum, was produced in small numbers, but was not a success; it was almost twice the size of the normal drum, but only held 12 more rounds. This drum seems to be the cause of the occasional references to a '200-round High Speed AA drum' encountered in the secondary literature, presumably on the basis that it was so much larger than the usual 100-round drum. So far as the author has been able to determine, no 200-round drum for the Bren was ever put into production.

However, the Bren was actually a relatively poor AA weapon, for two reasons. First, its rate of fire (around 500rds/min, depending on version and gas setting) was rather too low to engage crossing aircraft, with the gun only firing about eight bullets during the half a second or so when the aircraft was in the sights. By contrast, the German MG 42, which had been expressly designed with a much higher rate of fire (1,200rds/min) to allow AA fire, would fire 20 rounds in the same period. Various studies were made of ways to increase the Bren's rate of

Scots Guards with a Bren on the Mk 1 tripod in its anti-aircraft configuration, 1938. The men still wear service dress and 1908 Pattern webbing, a reminder that the classic look of the World War II British soldier was only just coming in as the war began. The tripod could also be set up for the ground role, without the extended AA leg. (IWM Army Training 1938 1/29)

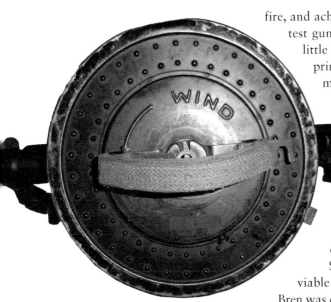

Top view of a Bren AA drum showing the webbing grip and arrow indicating the direction to wind up the drum's internal spring. (Author)

fire, and achieved a rate of fire of over 700rds/min from the test guns. However, it was strongly felt that this was a little high for an infantry gun, which was after all its primary role, and no further action was taken. While mounting two guns together did help somewhat, it is worth remembering that at the point when the Bren was coming into service, the RAF was specifying *eight* of the high-speed version of the Browning .303in machine gun as the minimum armament for its new fighters, each firing at twice the rate of the Bren – a combined equivalent of around 9,000rds/min.

Second, while rifle-calibre bullets might have been viable against the aircraft of the early 1930s when the Bren was designed, aircraft design moved on during the war. Cockpits and fuel tanks were commonly armoured, and aircraft guns increasingly moved to .50in calibre, or even 20mm. This meant that the .303in rounds from the Bren were significantly less likely to bring down an aircraft than the rounds from the .50in M2 machine gun the US Army used in the AA role, though in fairness this was a much heavier gun that could not have replaced the Bren.

Given this, it is perhaps fortunate that Allied air superiority after D-Day meant that the Bren saw little use in the AA role. Indeed, Allied troops were explicitly ordered NOT to fire at any aircraft for much of the campaign, after the RAF and USAAF complained of frequently taking ground fire from Allied units despite the black-and-white 'invasion stripes' painted on their aircraft to avoid such incidents.

Despite this, the Bren continued in the AA role after World War II; the six-wheeled Saracen APC that served through the 1960s had an AA Bren on a ring mount over the infantry compartment as well as its turreted Browning. Given that the targets by that point would have been Soviet jets, one may feel that this was slightly optimistic. No drum magazines were produced or adapted for the 7.62mm NATO versions of the Bren.

The Bren as a tank gun

The original specification for the Bren paid very little attention to its possible use as a tank gun. Partly, this is because when the specification was developed, the British Army was not mechanized, and still relied on mounted units for traditional cavalry roles such as reconnaissance. Even those who believed the tank was the weapon of the future, rather than a one-off response to the unique conditions of the Western Front, were not sure of the role or design of future tanks.

Previous British tanks had used the various British machine guns in service (Vickers, Lewis and Hotchkiss) without significant modification, so it was not really appreciated that tank use really had any particular

A Bren in the cramped turret of a Humber Light Reconnaissance Car. The turret on this vehicle was open-topped to allow the Bren to be used against aircraft as well as ground targets, but gives an idea of how awkward it would have been to use it as a vehicle co-axial gun on tanks or similar vehicles. (IWM H 25271)

A Universal Carrier of The Duke of Cornwall's Light Infantry, 1940. This vehicle has its Bren gun on the AA pedestal mount and its Boys .55in anti-tank rifle in the firing port in the front plate. It was also common to mount the Bren in the latter location, however, particularly later in the war when the Boys was no longer effective against improved enemy armour. (IWM H 4954)

requirements, and indeed, the ZGB was described as 'A most promising weapon for use in the Royal Tank Corps' (SAC 1420) in a 1935 minute from the RTC gunnery school. Unfortunately, the machine guns in previous British tanks had been installed in dedicated mounts with an individual gunner for each machine gun. Things were very different in the tanks of World War II, where the machine gun was often mounted in a much tighter space as a co-axial weapon next to the main armament.

The Bren quickly proved unsuitable for this role. Its top-mounted magazine limited the angle of depression possible in a fixed mounting, its magazine capacity was too small and too awkward to change in a confined space, and it relied on a quick-change barrel for sustained fire. As a result, the British Army adopted a second Czech design, the Zb 53, as the Besa tank gun. It was a belt-fed weapon with a heavier barrel. It was a solid and dependable weapon that served as a co-axial gun on British tanks through to the A34 Comet, but obviously, having multiple designs in service complicated spare-part supply and training.

To make things worse, the Lend-Lease tanks supplied by the United States (such as the M4 Sherman) that made up a significant part of the British tank fleet used yet another design (the .30in M1919 Browning) as their co-axial weapon. It was not until the adoption of the L7A1 GPMG that the British Army finally got one gun which could fulfil both the infantry and tank roles adequately, and even then, Browning guns soldiered on in service aboard older types such as the Ferret and Saracen into the 1970s.

The Bren was a perfectly viable gun on open-topped vehicles, such as the Daimler Dingo scout car and Universal Carrier. Indeed, it became so closely associated with the latter vehicle that it was almost universally known as the 'Bren Gun Carrier'.

OTHER USERS

While the service history above has concentrated on the British and Commonwealth forces that were the main users of the weapon, other forces also used the Bren.

The Middle East wars

Jewish irregular groups such as Haganah used Brens stolen from British forces in attacks against British troops administering the League of Nations mandate in Palestine, and against Palestinian Arabs they believed were attacking Jewish communities, attempting to drive them out so that a Jewish homeland could be established in Israel. When the United Nations resolved to set up such a state in 1947, Israel's Arab neighbours objected to the resulting partition of Palestine, and invaded the new state within hours of its independence in 1948. Both Arab and Israeli forces in the 1948 war used Brens as their primary LMG, and some remained in service with the Israeli Defence Forces into the 1956 war, after which they were generally replaced by the Belgian FN MAG.

Irish troops in the Congo

The Irish Army adopted largely British-manufactured weapons, and Irish troops were equipped with Bren guns as support weapons when they deployed as UN peacekeeping troops to the recently independent Republic of the Congo in 1960. Ethnic and political tensions in the former Belgian colony had led to civil unrest and the secession of the province of Katanga from what the UN recognized as the legitimate government.

A company of 155 Irish troops was besieged in the town of Jadotville by Katangese forces, under repeated attacks including air attacks by an aircraft piloted by a Belgian mercenary, and surrendered after six days when their ammunition ran out. Although these troops were later exchanged, ambushes against the Irish peacekeeping forces continued until the Katangese forces were defeated by the Congolese government in 1962. The most costly of these ambushes, at Niemba, saw an 11-man Irish patrol almost completely wiped out, despite killing almost three times their number of enemies with a Bren and a submachine gun. Irish forces had left the country before the 1964 rebellion, which led to the well-known parachute drop by Belgian para-commandos to rescue and evacuate western hostages from the region. The Bren was later replaced in Irish service by the FN MAG.

On the other side – Zb 26s in foreign service

As well as forming the basis for the British Bren, the Czech Zb 26 was itself purchased by a number of other countries, including Bolivia (who used it in the Gran Chaco war of the 1930s), Ethiopia (whose forces used it against the invading Italians) and Turkey.

The Zb 26 and its successor, the Zb 30, were also used by the forces of several of the Axis Powers. Romania produced the design under licence, and it was used by Romanian forces fighting alongside the Germans on the Eastern Front. Meanwhile, thousands of Czech guns, captured when the Nazis annexed that country and already chambered for the same 7.92mm Mauser cartridge used by the Wehrmacht, were taken into German service as the MG 26(t) and MG 30(t), respectively. Most went to the Waffen-SS, who had a lower priority for supply than the Heer (German Army) at this early stage of the war. The Germans continued to run the Brno factory throughout the war, producing Zb 30 guns both for themselves and for allies such as Franco's Spain, who received 20,000 guns.

The Nationalist Chinese bought a considerable number of Zb 26 guns, and ultimately set up several factories to produce the weapon. These were initially used both during the civil war and against the invading Japanese. After the communist takeover of China, they were used against United Nations forces by Chinese troops during the Korean War. The Chinese also supplied examples to the Vietnamese communist forces, which were used against first French and then American forces.

ABOVE Waffen-SS troops with a Zb 30 LMG; this is evidently a training photograph, as the usual muzzle cone has been replaced by a cylindrical blank-firing attachment. (IWM MH 1912)

The Germans also put actual Brens captured in action into use as the 7.7mm Leichte MG 138(e). By contrast, the Allies explicitly prohibited their troops from using captured machine guns, since the MG 34 and particularly the MG 42 made a very distinctive 'ripping cloth' noise due to their high rate of fire; any other Allied troops hearing it tended to pour fire at the source of the sound without waiting to see who was firing the gun.

The last time that British troops faced Zb-series weapons was in Afghanistan, where a Turkish-made Zb 30 was captured by British forces in 2009, 70-odd years after it was produced. The gun is now held at the Small Arms School Museum in Warminster, Wiltshire.

The India–Pakistan wars

Both the Indian and Pakistani armies were initially equipped with British equipment when the countries were partitioned on independence in 1947. Both thus used the Bren as their standard LMG in the 1947 war that broke out between the two when there was not a clear line between the Hindu and Muslim populations that the new border could follow, and over Kashmir, where the local ruler was allowed to choose which of the two states it joined. Both continued to use the Bren in the 1965 war, and in the case of Indian forces, for the 1971 war. A version of the Bren remained in production at the Ishapore arsenal as the MG1B until recently, and only began to be withdrawn from Indian service in 2012.

The Nigerian Civil War

Nigeria gained independence from Britain in 1960, but was a somewhat artificial entity, with tensions between the Muslim, traditionalist north and more westernized and Christian south. This led to ethnic violence and the breaking away of the south-eastern part of the country to form the state of Biafra in 1967. Nigerian forces were largely equipped with British small arms, including the Bren, during the war, which lasted until 1970, and some 7.62mm NATO Brens remained in service for a considerable time afterwards.

Grenada

In 1983, the pro-communist government of Grenada was deposed in a coup by hard-line elements of its own military, who executed the prime minister and a number of other ministers and government officials as well as firing on demonstrators. Concerned for the safety of over 1,000 US citizens on the island, the US government intervened, landing troops to take over the island and secure the medical school campus where most of the US citizens were located.

While the invasion itself was carried out by US forces, the United States was keen to avoid accusations of unilateralism by involving other Caribbean countries in the operation. Several countries therefore provided troops or police to assist with security after the invasion. This included contingents from Barbados and Jamaica, both of whom were photographed with the L4A2 Brens they had brought as support weapons.

IMPACT
Towards a GPMG

It is tempting to see something symbolic in the fact that the first British soldier to set foot on Occupied Europe on D-Day was a Bren gunner, Private William Gray of D Company, 2nd Battalion, The Oxfordshire & Buckinghamshire Light Infantry. He was part of the glider-borne force that landed at two minutes past midnight on 6 June to seize and hold the vital bridges across the River Orne and the Caen Canal. These provided the only exit eastwards for the British forces landing on Sword Beach to link up with 6th Airborne Division. In his own words:

A Scots Guardsman with his Bren stripped down to its major components for cleaning, Italy, April 1944. (IWM NA 14244)

Den Brotheridge, our platoon commander, quickly got the door open and said 'Gun out', which was me. Out I jumped, stumbled on the grass because of the weight I had on me, and set the Bren up facing the bridge and the rest of the lads jumped out. Den Brotheridge got in front of me and looked round to make sure that everyone was out and said 'Come on, lads'. We were about thirty yards from the bridge and we dashed towards it. I saw a German on the right-hand side and I let rip at him and down he went. I kept firing as I went over the bridge. On the other side was another German and he went down too. (Quoted in Bailey 2009: 121)

In fact, it was standard procedure for the first men off any transport in a combat situation to be the section Bren team, partly to get their firepower into action as quickly as possible, and partly because, as Lance-Corporal Thomas Packwood, another man in Gray's platoon, put it: 'You don't want a bloke firing from the hip with a Bren gun if you're in front of him' (Quoted in Bailey 2009: 123).

ACCURACY AND RELIABILITY

The Bren was generally an extremely accurate weapon, with each gun being rigorously tested for accuracy before it left the factory. Indeed, many gunners felt that the Bren was initially *too* accurate, as it tended to produce quite a narrow cone of fire, and thus a tight grouping of hits. While this is usually seen as a good thing when firing on a peacetime shooting range, it becomes less desirable in battle; when a burst was fired at a group of soldiers, one man would take all the hits, leaving the men on either side of him unhurt. This led to some gunners using worn-out barrels, which produced a wider cone of fire, until the barrels were redesigned on later guns. Accuracy was also affected when barrels started to overheat, but the Bren's quick-change barrel meant this could be rectified just by switching to the spare barrel.

Mk III and IV Brens, with their shorter and lighter barrels, were slightly less accurate than the earlier marks. However, given that they were primarily intended for jungle warfare where engagement ranges were likely to be short, this was not a significant issue.

A 3× telescopic sight,[6] the No. 32 Mk 1, was developed for the Bren gun, but very few were ever issued for use on Brens, and the mounting slot for it was abolished as one of the simplifications of the Mk I Bren to speed up production. Ironically, the No. 32 sight was mounted on a modified Lee-Enfield No. 4 to create the No. 4(T) sniping rifle that served through World War II and Korea. The same sight was used on re-barrelled versions of the same rifle to create the No. 4(T)'s replacement, the L42A1 sniping rifle, which served on into the 1980s, last seeing combat in the Falklands War.

After some initial teething troubles with early guns, the Bren acquired an enviable reputation for reliability. Detailed analysis of stoppages indicated that the most common cause of malfunction was defective ammunition, i.e. that the weapon was actually more reliable than the ammunition it was firing. The list of potential stoppages in the Bren manual included only eight items – mercifully short, particularly for veterans used to the much more stoppage-prone Lewis gun. The first and most common one was 'Empty magazine'. The 1939 version of the manual indicated that the NCO instructor should at this point 'Explain the effect of no ammunition in the magazine' (War Office 1939: 34). One can only imagine what a pre-war Regular British NCO would have said at that point, and it is perhaps significant that the next version of the manual assumes that this stoppage is self-explanatory. Recruits were taught a handy mnemonic to remember the stoppages:

6 '3×' indicates the magnifying power of the sight, and means that a target 600yd away will appear the same size as a target 200yd away seen with the naked eye.

England	Empty magazine
Breeds	Badly filled magazine
Many	Misfire
Fine	Faulty ejection
Horses	Hard extraction
In	Insufficient gas
Our	Obstruction in barrel
Shires	Split casing

Old soldiers often swore that as a rule of thumb, almost all Bren stoppages could be dealt with by changing the magazine, turning the four-position gas regulator above the bipod to the next bigger hole to use more gas to drive the action, or slapping the side of the gun.

THE BREN GUN AND MORALE

Weapons like the Bren are important because of their psychological, as well as their physical, impact on the battlefield. When Brigadier General S.L.A. Marshall, the official historian of the US Army, published his classic analysis of infantry combat after the war, one of the most striking points was that he believed that in a typical fire-fight, less than one man in four actually fired at the enemy (Marshall 1947: 50–51).

Marshall's methodology has been criticized subsequently, but most Western armies took it seriously enough to amend their training programmes based on his work, for instance replacing the traditional bullseye targets on firing ranges with man-shaped silhouettes to get troops used to shooting at things that looked like people. It is also striking that the audience he wrote for – US Army officers and NCOs, almost all combat veterans themselves – seem to have generally accepted his findings, and similar studies since have produced similar though not identical results.

The reasons for this failure to fire were not (as often assumed) simply because the remaining men were cowering behind cover for fear of return fire, but also included disorientation, not having a clear target, reluctance to kill and isolation from their comrades as men took cover from incoming fire. Interestingly, Marshall noted that men with support weapons such as BARs were much more likely to fire than their comrades with rifles, apparently because they believed that their firing – or not doing so – would have a greater effect on the outcome of the fight. Two or more men together were also much more likely to fire than single soldiers on their own, as were men under the direct supervision of an NCO.

If we accept Marshall's conclusions, this suggests that Bren teams – two men armed with a support weapon they have confidence in, and directly supervised by an NCO – are likely to have had an even greater relative effect on the battlefield than would be expected. Some Bren teams certainly achieved striking feats of determination. Private George Sands, a Bren gunner serving with 5th Cameron Highlanders, describes facing a German counter-attack with tanks and infantry shortly after D-Day:

I was firing the Bren, with Sandy reloading it with fresh clips of ammunition. But we could not halt the Germans' advance. They had set up a Spandau [MG 34 or MG 42] heavy machine-gun and were spraying our positions with heavy fire, inflicting casualties all around us. Sandy was just fitting a fresh clip of ammunition on the Bren when he took a full burst of machine-gun fire through his upper arm, tearing away most, if not all, of his flesh and muscle. I kept the gun firing and Sandy, I don't know how, kept reloading the Bren with his one good arm. (Renouf 2011: 102–04)

What Sands fails to say is that he himself had been badly wounded, in the face and both legs, by fire that had also torn the barrel off his Bren gun.

A Bren gunner from No. 9 Commando, near Anzio, Italy, in February or March 1944. Unusually, he is only wearing one ammunition pouch, plus a spare magazine tucked in to the top pocket of his battledress under his leather jerkin. Curiously, Commando Bren gunners were often seen carrying pistols. (IWM NA 12471)

Despite this, he kept the Bren in action using the spare barrel until the attack had been repulsed. He refused to be evacuated afterwards, and crawled with his gun to a position from which he could engage another expected attack, continuing to operate the Bren until the company withdrew. He was awarded the Military Medal for his actions.

Men did not always want to be Bren gunners. While the job had a certain prestige, it also meant extra hard work carrying the heavy gun and ammunition. The author's father, doing his basic training in the early 1960s, commented: 'I tried to avoid being in the section Bren team, as it involved carrying more weight and during section tactics you were doubling all over the place, as the section commander was always changing his orders as to whether he wanted the Bren to the left or right flank of the attack.'

It could also be a dangerous job, as enemy troops concentrated fire on Bren teams. George MacDonald Fraser, who served in Burma during 1945, described his fear as he moved to take up his section Bren after the gunner was hit, and his relief when another member of the section reached it first. It is worth noting, however, that Fraser *was* moving toward the fallen Bren, scared or not – the combat effectiveness and potentially the very survival of the section was too dependent on its firepower (Fraser 1993: 114).

TECHNICAL IMPACT

The majority of the Bren's design features were relatively conventional. The top-mounted magazine – easier to change while lying prone than the bottom-mounted magazine of the BAR and easier to carry than the pan magazines of the Lewis or Soviet DP – had already appeared on other guns, such as the Danish Madsen and the French FM 24/29.

A Rhodesian Bren gunner of the 60th (King's Royal Rifle Corps) during a training exercise, 1942. Despite the relatively late date, his Bren still has a rear handle fitted. (IWM E 11698)

The one radical design feature was the quick-change barrel. Its predecessor, the World War I-era Lewis gun, had a forced-air cooling sleeve around its fixed barrel. Even so, it started to overheat after firing 400–500 rounds in a reasonably short space of time. After that point, it started to lose accuracy and barrel wear increased dramatically as the steel of the barrel softened. If the gunner continued firing, the gun overheated to the point where it simply stopped firing, generally well before reaching 1,000 rounds. Fixed-barrel machine guns without the cooling sleeve of the Lewis, such as the BAR or the FM 24/29, reached this point earlier, in some cases after as little as 500 rounds.[7]

By contrast, the quick-change barrel on the Bren meant that the crew could simply swap to the spare barrel after 300 rounds and keep on firing while the first barrel cooled. Given a sufficient supply of spare barrels, the Bren could keep on firing more or less indefinitely. Even under combat conditions with only one spare barrel, it was unusual for a Bren team to overheat their gun to the point where barrel wear became an issue.

---

7   Some have questioned whether the cooling sleeve on the Lewis gun made any difference, since a large number of aerial Lewis guns (with the cooling sleeves removed) were pressed into ground service during World War II, and worked perfectly well. This is to miss the point, however; the Lewis does not need the cooling sleeve in order to function, any more than other air-cooled machine guns such as the Browning M1919. However, by increasing the airflow over the barrel, it improved cooling so that the Lewis can remain in operation longer before overheating.

A quick-change barrel was not unique to the Bren: the Belgian firm of FN had been producing a version of the BAR with a quick-change barrel, and quick-change barrels were a key feature of the German MG 34 and its successor, the MG 42. However, the Bren barrel design was better than either, since it could be done in only a few seconds by a well-trained crew, and the carrying handle attached to the barrel meant that the changeover could be accomplished without the felt pads required by the MG 34 design.

This quick-change barrel design was copied by the Bren's replacement, the very widely adopted FN MAG. It is perhaps unfortunate that the US Army was so impressed by the MG 42 that they essentially copied its barrel change for their postwar M60 along with its belt-feed mechanism, rather than adopting a Bren-type design, thus forcing US machine-gunners to carry an asbestos glove to handle the hot barrels safely.

The Bren was manufactured to a high standard even in its simplified versions, giving excellent accuracy and reliability. However, high-quality production is not always an unmitigated virtue in wartime, if it slows down getting weapons into the hands of the troops, and the Bren was in desperately short supply in the early days of the war. Britain was fortunate that she was able to obtain substitute guns to see her troops through the worst, and was able to call on the manufacturing resources of the Commonwealth, particularly Canada, to help with this production bottleneck.

A Bren gunner demonstrates the position for firing in the assault as he charges through a stream during training in the UK, 1941. (IWM H 11837)

The fact remains, however, that the Bren was somewhat over-engineered. Its receiver was machined from high-grade steel to give a life of five million rounds, and other main components had also been designed for long working lives by men thinking in terms of the vast ammunition consumption of World War I machine guns. In practice, very few Brens fired anything like that number of rounds. Even those weapons in constant use were far more likely to be irreparably damaged by enemy fire than they were to wear out. Combined with an organized programme of factory overhaul, this meant that very substantial numbers of wartime and later Brens had plenty of working life still in them when they were replaced by the L7A1 GPMG.

Whether the Bren could have been redesigned to trade off a shorter working life for reduced weight and ease of production without compromising accuracy and reliability is a moot point; as the fate of the Besal design indicated, there was little appetite for such a project once the initial crisis of supply had passed.

TACTICAL IMPACT

The Bren was originally intended to replace both the existing Lewis LMG and the heavier Vickers MMG, effectively serving as a GPMG in the same way as the German MG 34. Interestingly, although the Bren replaced both guns, it was only expected to cover 75 per cent of the roles performed by the Vickers. The remaining 25 per cent largely related to the indirect-fire role, and would be taken over by the battalion mortar platoon, a weapon not available when the Vickers was first introduced.

The Bren fulfilled the first part of the requirement very effectively, completely replacing the Lewis in all roles, and was almost universally agreed to perform them better. The second part is less clear-cut. The Bren on a tripod mount did take over many of the roles of the Vickers, but did not replace it completely; instead, the Vickers gun soldiered on through World War II and Korea, with the last not leaving front-line service until 1968. One cannot help wondering, however, how much this was simply because existing Vickers guns were available and did the job; one of the reasons why the MG 34 was used in all roles across the Wehrmacht is because the Treaty of Versailles had stripped the German Army of its existing stocks of Maxim MG 08s.

On the other hand, while the Bren did largely replace the two machine guns already in service with the British Army, the war saw several more machine guns adopted, notably the Besa and Browning M1919, which came into service as vehicle guns because of the Bren's limitations in that role. It is perhaps unreasonable to blame the Bren for not meeting requirements that did not exist when it was adopted, however. The Bren's success as a 'universal gun' must, therefore, be somewhat qualified. Only the Germans managed to produce such a gun in World War II, however, and the Bren is generally held to have performed excellently in the light role.

The British Army had experimented with using motorcycle combinations to move machine guns since World War I. The idea saw little use after 1940, however, as the Universal Carrier effectively fulfilled the role instead. (IWM H 5979)

Adoption of the Bren marked a clear shift in British small-unit tactics. After the Lewis began to be issued at platoon level during World War I, British platoons were organized as four specialized sections (one section each of riflemen, 'bombers' with hand grenades, rifle grenadiers and the Lewis gun section). From 1918 until the adoption of the Bren, each platoon was organized as two Lewis gun sections and two rifle sections. The smaller six-man Lewis sections existed to support the rifle sections, and were not generally split down further. Instead, the riflemen in them primarily served to carry the very large amount of ammunition that the doctrine of the period believed necessary – 44 47-round pans, a total of more than 2,000 rounds, twice that carried for the Bren and far more than the Lewis could actually fire in any sensible time without overheating.

By contrast, after the adoption of the Bren gun, the platoon was reorganized into three equal sections, each including both riflemen and a machine-gun team. The function of the riflemen was now to support and protect the machine gun, however, a reversal of roles compared to the Lewis. Each of the new sections could (and routinely was) split down into a gun group and a rifle group, so that the smallest unit capable of conducting fire and manoeuvre on its own was now the section, rather than the platoon as previously.

This organization of the platoon into three sections, each including a machine gun, remained the standard British Army organization well after the Bren had been replaced by the GPMG, with the new guns simply replacing the old without tactical or organizational change. It was only

with the arrival of the L85 assault rifle and its companion L86 LSW that the platoon was reorganized. After that point, each of the three sections was made up of two equal four-man 'bricks', each with an LSW and three riflemen, plus a GPMG on a sustained-fire tripod as part of platoon HQ.

The 'section machine gun' idea may look obvious in retrospect, but in fact, it was only the Germans (the other combatant equipped with a GPMG) who adopted the concept during World War II. It is instructive to use the US Army as a comparison. During World War II, it provided each of its 12-man rifle squads with initially one BAR (and later two), but this was a significantly less capable weapon than the Bren, being lighter than its British counterpart but at the cost of offering a much-reduced sustained-fire capability; the closest equivalent US weapon to the Bren (the .30in Browning M1919) was held at platoon level or higher. Once the BAR and M1 Garand were replaced by the M14 and later the M16, the only machine guns in a US infantry platoon were two M60s in the platoon HQ, parcelled out as the platoon commander felt necessary. Individual US squads did not routinely have an organic machine gun until the adoption of the 5.56mm M249 Squad Automatic Weapon in the 1980s.

US Marine Corps organization was slightly different, since they increased the number of BARs in their squads first to two and then three weapons, so that the 12-man squad was split into three four-man fire teams, each with a BAR – an organization oddly reminiscent of that used by the British after the change to the L86 LSW, a weapon perhaps closer to the BAR than the Bren.

The Navy also used Brens, as secondary armament on smaller vessels and as part of the armament of boarding and security parties for larger ones, such as this sailor aboard a battleship. It isn't clear how he will carry magazines for his Bren in his World War I-era 1908 Pattern webbing, however. (IWM TR 325)

IMPACT ON THE ENEMY

All versions of the Bren, whether chambered for .303in or 7.62mm NATO, fired a full-power rifle cartridge that propelled a relatively heavy bullet with significant range and muzzle velocity. However, while the Bren provided most of the firepower of the rifle section, bullets were not the main killer on the battlefields of World War II.

The British Army analysed casualties caused during the war, largely in order to evaluate the utility of proposals to introduce body armour. They found that approximately 40 per cent of casualties were caused by 'fine fragmenting' weapons such as grenades and mortars, 25 per cent by 'coarse fragmenting' weapons such as artillery and tank shells, and only the remaining 35 per cent by 'bullets and other causes'. This is broadly consistent with the official estimate of 60 per cent of World War I casualties being caused by artillery and trench mortars.

Even allowing that 'other causes' – which covered wounds inflicted by everything from bayonets to flamethrowers – was a relatively small component of the 35 per cent, and that the majority of the bullet casualties were inflicted by machine guns rather than rifles, the actual number of casualties inflicted by machine gun weapons was often overestimated.

The Lewis gun had been known to German troops of World War I as 'The Belgian Rattlesnake', but no Allied machine gun of World War II acquired a nickname among enemy troops, in the way that the German MG 42 was sometimes known as 'Hitler's Buzzsaw' and similar epithets. None appeared to arouse the same degree of fear among opponents as the German gun did among Allied infantrymen.

The Bren gun in film and television

The Bren gun can be relied upon to make an appearance whenever World War II-era British troops are shown on film or television, its distinctive curved magazine acting as an easy visual cue.

It was used in many of the big-budget Anglo-American war films popular in the 1960s and 1970s, such as *The Guns of Navarone* (1961), *The Longest Day* (1962), *A Bridge Too Far* (1977) and *The Wild Geese* (1978). It appeared less on screen during the 1980s and 1990s, as World War II was replaced by Vietnam as the most common backdrop for war films. By the time World War II was re-popularized by Steven Spielberg's *Saving Private Ryan* in 1998, the balance of power in the film industry had swung firmly toward Hollywood, and the majority of World War II movies made since that point, such as *Pearl Harbor* and *Flags of Our Fathers*, have been dominated by American characters and equipment.

It is something of an oddity that Britain never produced a television series about troops fighting in World War II, along the lines of the long-running US series *Combat!*, or the later *Band of Brothers* and *The Pacific*. Instead, British television has generally looked at the war through the prism of comedy, in series such as the very successful *Dad's Army*, *'Allo 'Allo!* and *It Ain't Half Hot Mum*. In the cases where the war has been treated as drama, it has usually involved the Resistance (*Secret Army*) or prisoners of war (*Tenko*, *Colditz*), rather than troops on the front lines.

The Bren has also turned up in some very strange places, being wielded by homicidal schoolgirls in the 1960s comedy *The Pure Hell of St. Trinian's*, by Malcolm McDowell's equally homicidal public schoolboy in the 1968 surrealist film *if....* and perhaps most bizarrely in the 1998 gangster movie *Lock, Stock and Two Smoking Barrels*.

CONCLUSION

The Bren could make a legitimate claim to be the first true GPMG, intended to replace both the Lewis gun and the heavier Vickers. However, it never completely filled this aspiration, and the title is perhaps best left

An Australian Bren gunner moving through the bush in New Guinea, May 1944. (AWM 073277)

to the German MG 34 (adopted as a service weapon before the Bren was, but having its origins in the Solothurn MG 30, a weapon developed some time after the Bren's ancestor, the Zb 26). This should not take anything away from the Bren's very real strengths. It was probably the best light machine gun of its generation, easily outperforming rivals such as the French FM 24/29 or the Soviet DP.

It served three generations of British and Commonwealth soldiers faithfully, from North West Europe to the South Atlantic and from the British Isles to Burma and Korea. It carried on working in environments as different as the burning sands of the Western Desert, the snow and ice of the Norwegian campaign and the mud and rain of the Falklands. It outlasted the .303in round it was originally chambered for, and continued in service in specialized roles long after it had been replaced in general service, and well after almost all of its rivals had been consigned to museums.

During six decades of service, it acquired an impressive reputation for reliability, durability and accuracy. It was not a perfect weapon. However, any machine-gun design must inevitably make compromises between incompatible factors. A high rate of fire, for example, might be excellent for anti-aircraft work but impractical in an infantry gun, while making components lighter to reduce weight may also make them less rugged and more likely to break.

The Bren can fairly claim to have been an excellent set of compromises, giving superlative performance compared to weight and cost of manufacture. It did not excel in all areas – as a vehicle gun, for example – but no other gun of its era successfully filled all roles, either. At the last, the most important opinion of a weapon must be that of the men who carried it into combat. It is striking that almost none of the men who did so had a bad word to say about the Bren, remembering it with almost universal affection and respect.

BIBLIOGRAPHY

Bailey, Roderick, *Forgotten Voices of D-Day*, London, Ebury (2009)

Chappell, Mike, *The British Soldier in the 20th Century: 4 – Light Machine Guns*, Okehampton, Wessex Publishing (1988)

Dugelby, Thomas B., *The Bren Gun Saga*, Ontario, Collector's Grade Publications (1999)

Fraser, George MacDonald, *Quartered Safe Out Here*, London, HarperCollins (1993)

Hobart, Major F.W.A., *Small Arms Profile 13: The Bren Gun*, London, Profile Publications (1972)

Khan, Mark, 'The Bren Gun' in *Britain at War*, Issue 21, January 2009 (2009), pp.47–52

Levine, Joshua, *Forgotten Voices of Dunkirk*, London, Ebury (2010)

Marshall, S.L.A., *Men Against Fire: The Problem of Battle Command*, New York, NY, William Morrow & Co (1947)

Renouf, Tom, *Black Watch*, London, Little, Brown (2011)

Salmon, Andrew, *To the Last Round: The Epic British stand on the Imjin River, Korea 1951*, London, Aurum (2009)

Small Arms Committee minute 1108, November 1930

Small Arms Committee minute 1188, November 1931

Small Arms Committee minute 1420, March 1935

Small Arms Committee minute 1544, December 1935

Thompson, Julian, *Forgotten Voices – Desert Victory*, London, Ebury (2010)

War Office, *War Office Papers 20/Inf/2024* (1930)

War Office, *Infantry Training (1937)*, London, HMSO (1937)

War Office, *Small Arms Training, Vol. 1, Pamphlet No. 4 – Light Machine Gun 1939*, London, HMSO (1939)

War Office, *Infantry Training Part V – The Carrier Platoon 1943*, London, HMSO (1943)

War Office, *Infantry Training Part VIII – Fieldcraft, Battle Drill, Section & Platoon Tactics*, London, HMSO (1944)

War Office, *Infantry Notes 1945*, London, HMSO (1945)

War Office, *The .303 Bren Light Machine-Gun (1939, 1942 and Home Guard Pamphlets)*, London, Military Library Research Services (2005). Originally published in 1939 and 1942

INDEX